cats
up close

Cats up close

Vicki Croke

ARTABRAS

A Division of Abbeville Publishing Group

New York • London • Paris

contents

introduction

What do we see when we look at cats up close?

Jeweled eyes. Slender, sleek, strong bodies. Affectionate, trusting souls. Independence. Sophistication. A spirit both wise and wiseacre.

Whether the cat by our side is a long hair, short hair, tabby, or tortoiseshell, we experience the same reaction: enchantment. Mysterious and elegant, playful and tender, cats are the most beguiling creatures our species has brought in from the cold.

But throughout history, cats have been a conundrum for societies. Secretive or sweet? Solitary or sociable? Spiritual or sinister? Physically, cats have not changed very much at all, but our perceptions of them have.

Unlike the dog (how unlike the dog!), one of the earliest domesticated animals, cats came to us relatively late. But they have more than made up for lost time, quickly taking up position not just in our homes, but in our hearts.

And we have marauding rodents to thank.

It was the advent of agriculture, and with it stores of grain, that brought us our sophisticated and predatory pals, probably more than three thousand years ago. It is believed that the African wild cat was employed in ancient Egypt to dispatch the mice and rodents of the Nile Valley who were siphoning off harvested grain stored in silos.

The ancient Egyptians did not stand a chance once they had lived with these dazzling creatures: they were spellbound. The cats adored by the ancient Egyptians were very much the cats we adore today. Art from this time depicts the cat just the way we see it in our living rooms, although then there was perhaps a bit more pomp surrounding the celebration of things feline.

The Egyptians worshipped a cat goddess named Bastet. She rode a chariot drawn by other cats (most of us can imagine our own cats choosing others from the neighborhood to be harnessed—"that snooping little calico from Oak Street . . . the big burly Tom from the backyard . . ."). Bastet was a powerful goddess closely related to the sun god Re. Cats roamed a stone temple built in her honor and devotees studied their behavior for signs and signals from the great goddess herself. (We can, again, identify with these ancient Egyptians when we study our own cat's behavior for signals— "the salmon supreme or turkey giblet tonight? Give me a sign!"). In life, cats were loved; in death, they were mourned. If the household cat died, every-one in the Egyptian family would shave off their eyebrows.

But being worshipped is not always what it's cracked up to be, particularly in the twentieth century. In the United States, fifty-five million pampered cats have homes, while millions of others, unwanted, are euthanized every year. In Egypt, though the cat was held sacred, thousands were sacrificed and mummified. In one great temple, about three hundred thousand of these cat mummies, accompanied by a sort of bag lunch—mummified mice—were discovered just before the turn of the century.

Over several centuries, Bastet became more popular and powerful, drawing hundreds of thousands of promiscuous pilgrims to festivals celebrated with drinking, feasting, and wild sexual orgies. This history, along with nocturnal wanderings, reflective retinas that cause their eyes to "glow" in the dark, and the cat's natural pride (read as haughtiness), may have led to a shift in public opinion. Cats experienced dark times in medieval Europe, where they were linked to sorcery and witchcraft, and persecuted for hundreds of years because of this association. Though anti-cat hysteria began as early as the tenth century, the last cat known to be executed for sorcery in England died in 1712. And though we now understand what great companionship and solace cats can bring to the elderly, this precious relationship was misunderstood and destroyed during the Middle Ages, when an old, solitary woman who communed with cats was always suspected of sorcery.

Black cats were especially singled out during witch hunts, and the superstition surrounding them still exists. In the United States, a black cat crossing one's path is supposed to mean bad luck, but in England it portends the opposite—trouble passed by without touching you—and is good luck.

Throughout even the darkest times writers remained cats' allies, as both shared a love of solitude and quiet. For example, Trecento Italian poet Petrarch (who inscribed on his cat's grave marker, "I was the greatest passion, second only to Laura") and sixteenth-century French essayist Michel de Montaigne ("When I am playing with my cat, who knows whether she has more sport in dallying with me, than I have in gaming with her?") remained loyal. And this relationship has continued through countless generations. Cats have gracefully made the transition from quill to laptop computer. Keats, Tennyson, Hardy, Twain, Kipling, and Colette loved cats and wrote fondly about them. It will come as no surprise to anyone who has witnessed the breathtaking athleticism of common cats that ultra-macho writer Ernest Hemingway was a true cat lover.

And he is hardly alone. It is that sleek muscularity that attracts so many of us. Despite domestication, cats have changed relatively little. We do not see in them the marked physical differences between the wild and domesticated varieties that we do in other "beasts of burden" (just try applying that term to your cat).

More than any other domesticated species, our little Muffy and Lulu can survive on their own. The ball of fluff purring on your warm lap knows very well how to snag a meal from the great outdoors—whether in a meadow or the mean streets of Manhattan.

In those deep, gorgeous eyes of azure blue or emerald green or warm amber we can glimpse the wild. With acute night vision, hearing tuned in to high-pitched sound, and a sense of smell thirty times better than our own, cats are built for predation. Whether country- or city-bound, cats who are allowed outdoors establish territories. They use scent to mark boundaries and employ brawn to enforce them (though threats usually do the trick).

Even the tiniest kittens are born with hunting instructions included. They have natural predatory instincts and hone their skills through play with their littermates. If you've seen them bat and bite, you know they are practicing for scrumptious, live mice. By watching a parent, they learn patience, pouncing technique, and how to deliver the predatory bite to the neck. The hunting instinct is strong; lacking a mouse, toes under a blanket, slippers slapping the floor, or a trailing shoelace will do.

Some domesticated cats hear the call of the wild. They revert to nature and are able to feed themselves with captured birds and rodents. They often reproduce prolifically, but tend to live to only half the age of a pampered house cat. In many cities, welfare groups work to sterilize and immunize stable feral cat populations.

And there is great controversy about whether cats should be allowed outdoors at all. Most animal protection groups say that cats should be kept indoors at all times, citing statistics that show how drastically life expectancy is reduced the moment a cat pads outdoors.

The age-old question for the owner is, "What makes my cat happy?" We know they are sensitive to touch, and they react with their entire bodies to our caresses. They shiver with delight and pass their heads and backs and rumps under our palms. Many cats find ecstasy in catnip—rolling and rubbing in it with wild abandon.

Their pleasures seem to come from simple things. A sun-drenched pocket of the room. A paper bag. The feel of their claws in upholstery. Marathon naps. Respect—all right, worship—from others.

Cats are curious and complex. Loving but independent. Domesticated but wild. Aloof and attentive. Felines are so many things that the only way to really catalog their stories is through pictures. No matter which type of cat is shown or where the photo was taken, you will recognize your own cat— its universal feline essence—in each shot.

cats for all seasons

Though they would rather we did not know this fact, cats are rather hardy creatures. They are able to meet the changing seasons with robust metabolisms and are shrewd about finding both warm places in the winter and cool spots in the summer.

Still, most of us know "the look" only too well. We open the door for the cat one snowy afternoon, and after taking a peek at the snow outside she sullenly holds us responsible. Yet usually they head out anyway. And what a picture we see as they enter the outdoor realm.

Each season frames our beautiful cats in rich new colors. The lush greens of summer combined with bright sunlight makes eyes glow and coats glisten. Autumn leaves, winter snows, and spring rains invite different moods and include shadings from varied palettes.

Whatever the season, we know that cats adore warmth, whether it involves lying in pools of sunlight in summer or curling up by a fire in winter. It can even alarm cat owners to see their pets so close to such intense heat, but their noses and lips act as little thermometers, warning them to get up and move away if it really gets too hot.

Cats can be found throughout the world and can live comfortably anywhere, from the steamy equator to the frigid subantarctic. Thick coats and quick wits keep feral cats warm in colder climes. In equatorial heat, cats have thinner coats and can rid themselves of excess heat through sweat glands in the feet.

But why get overheated? Cats are quite shrewd about this. They work very hard, as we all know, to avoid overheating altogether.

And what does working hard at staying cool mean, exactly? Well, of course it means plenty of naps and slow movements in summer. (Naps seem to cure all kinds of problems, whatever the season.) In the fall, the chill puts a snap into their step (but still, plenty of time for napping) and through winter many are content to curl up under the blankets with us. We lose them a bit in the spring once again, as birds and bugs and blossoms take their thoughts elsewhere.

Whatever the time of year, wherever we are, we know that a home sis always a cozier place with a cat.

The wild beauty of cats allows us to look into the eyes of nature itself.

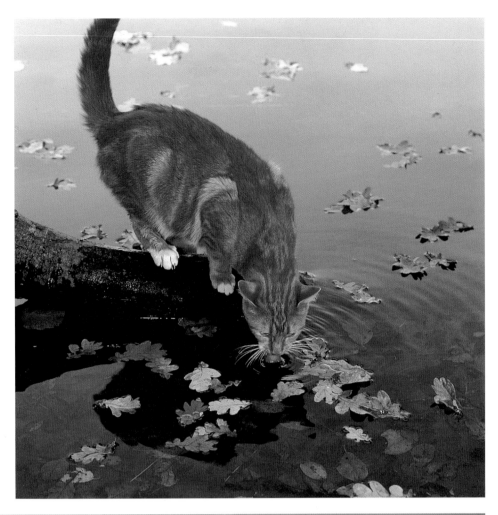

Drinking in the fall foliage. The feline tongue curls backward to form a ladle for drinking water.

In the fall grass: slinky, sleek, and alert, some domestic cats let us take a alk on the wild side.

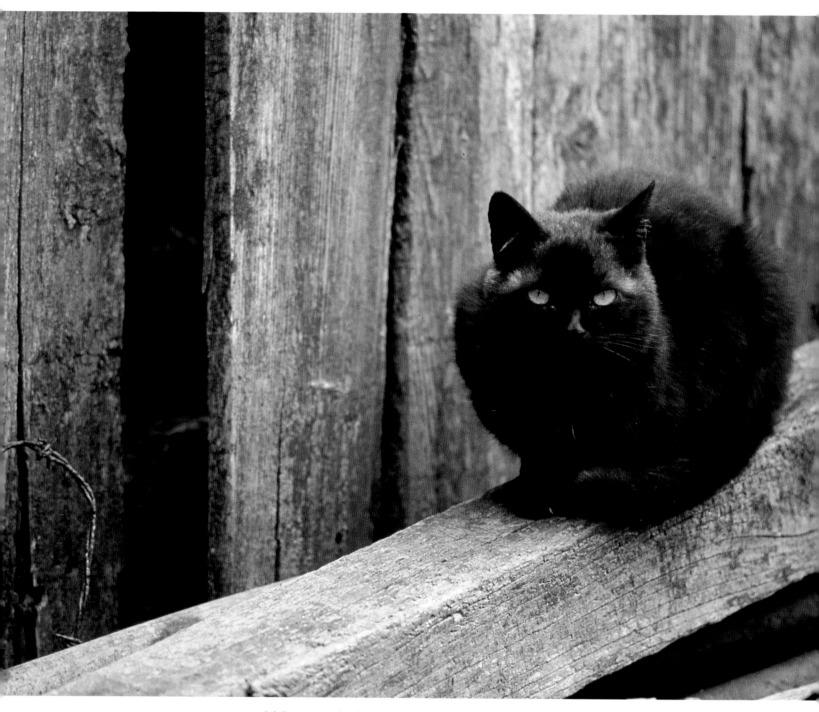

When cats look into our eyes, what do they see?

cats for all seasons

cats for all seasons

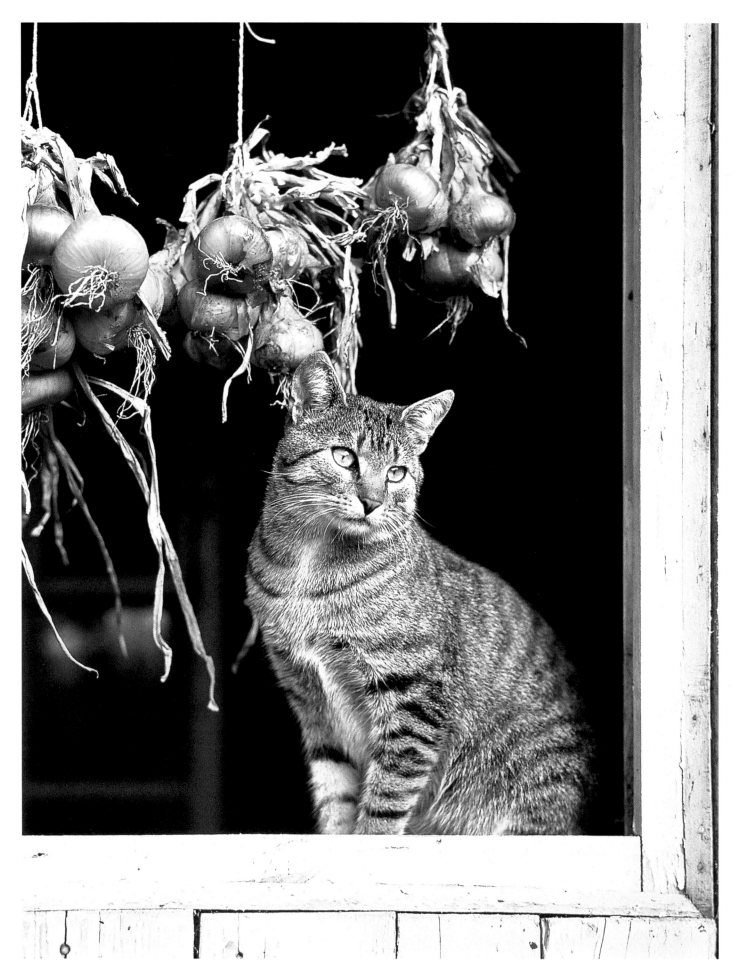

The wise cat stocks winter provisions.

cats for all seasons

Do you hear
what I hear?

Like finding a feline in a haystack.

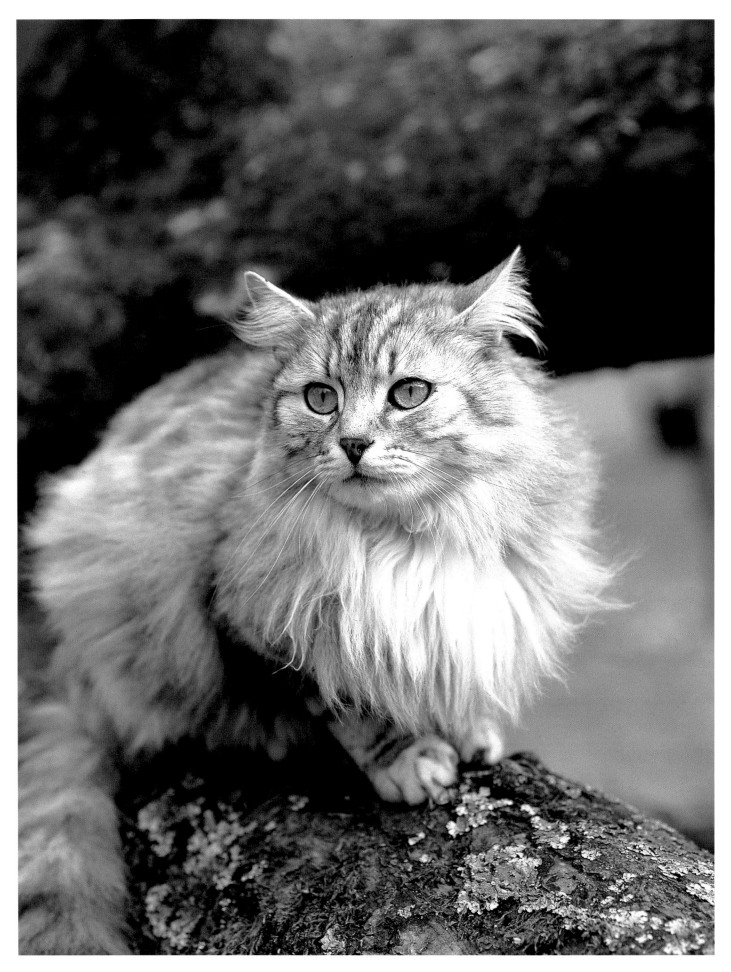

Profiles in furrage.

cats for all seasons

Wild life on the forest floor.

The belly roll display is a friendly and trusting greeting.

I can see clearly now, the pane is gone.

The shadows grow longer, the days
grow shorter, but cats remain consistent.

To every season, turn, turn, turn.

Snowy peaks.

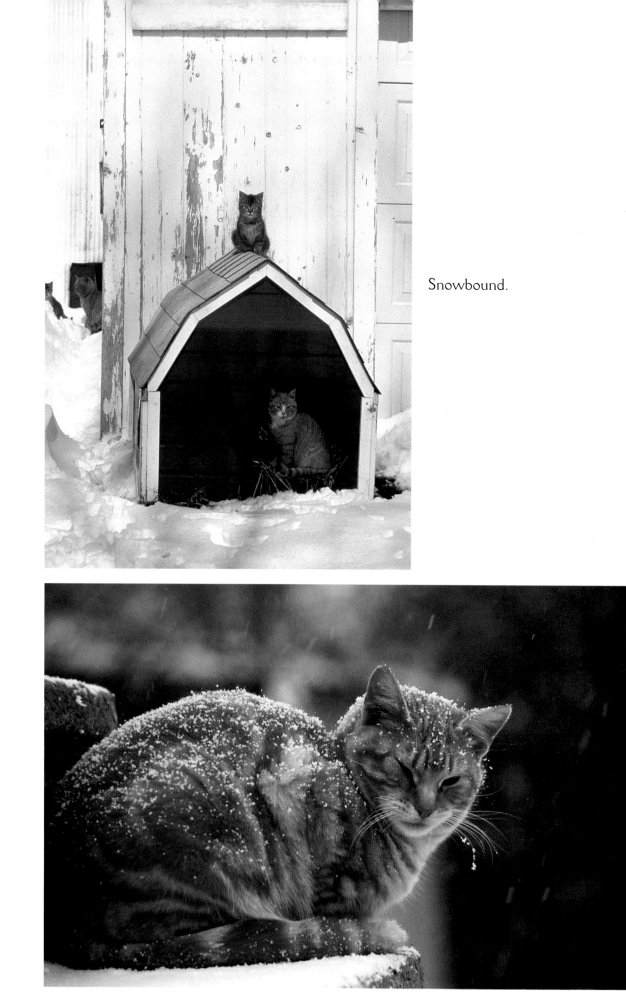

Snowbound.

Let it snow.

cats for all seasons

There's a little Siberian tiger in many a household cat . . .

. . . and a bit of jungle cat in many more.

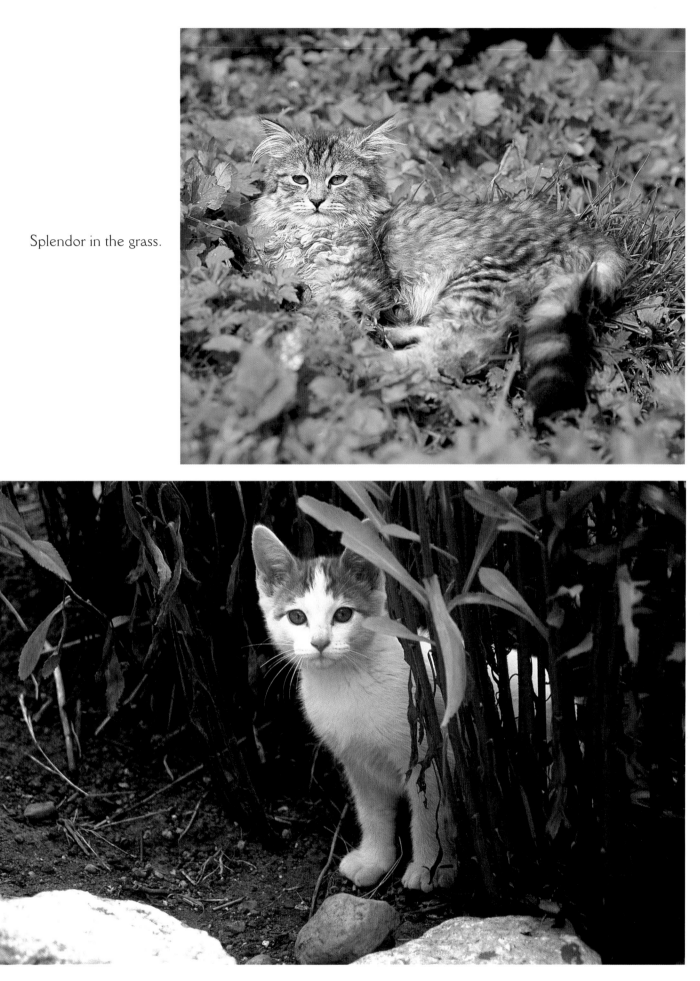

Splendor in the grass.

It's a jungle out here—and I love it.

The spring vegetation can—almost—hide a white cat.

cats for all seasons

Kittens' curiosity.   The lush life.

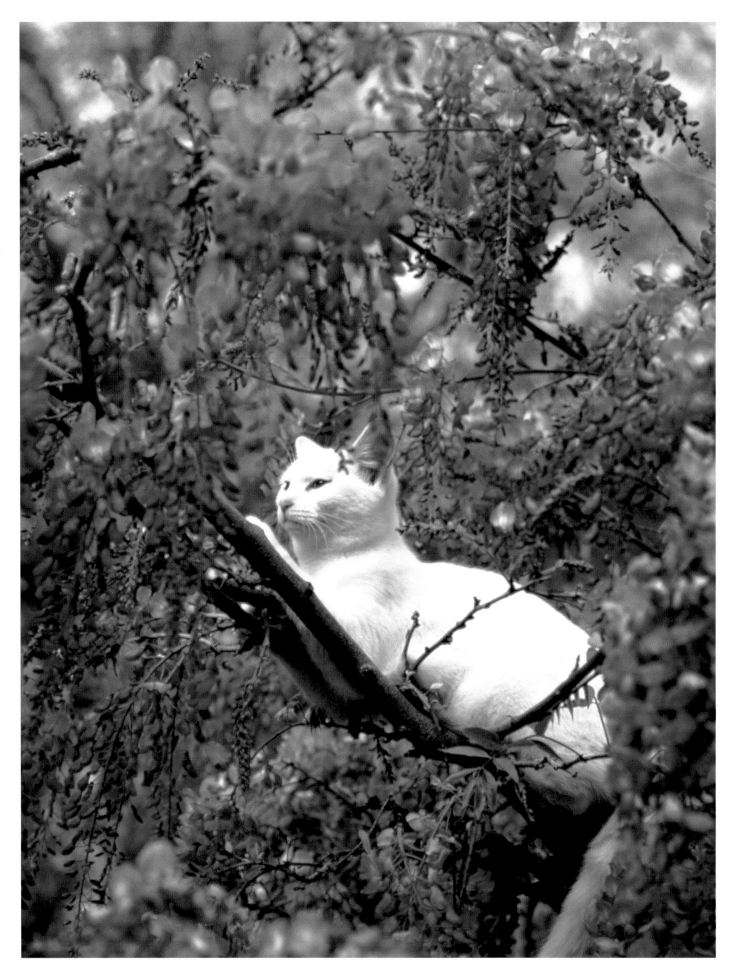

Royal purple for a regal cat.

cats for all seasons

Kittens in a basket.

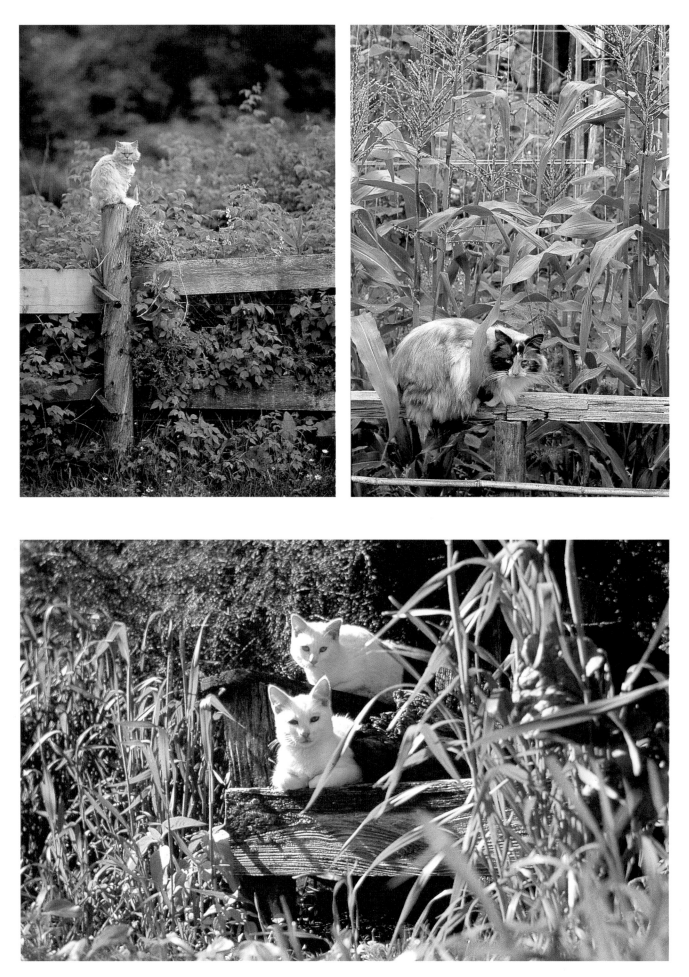

Taking in the landscape.

cats for all seasons

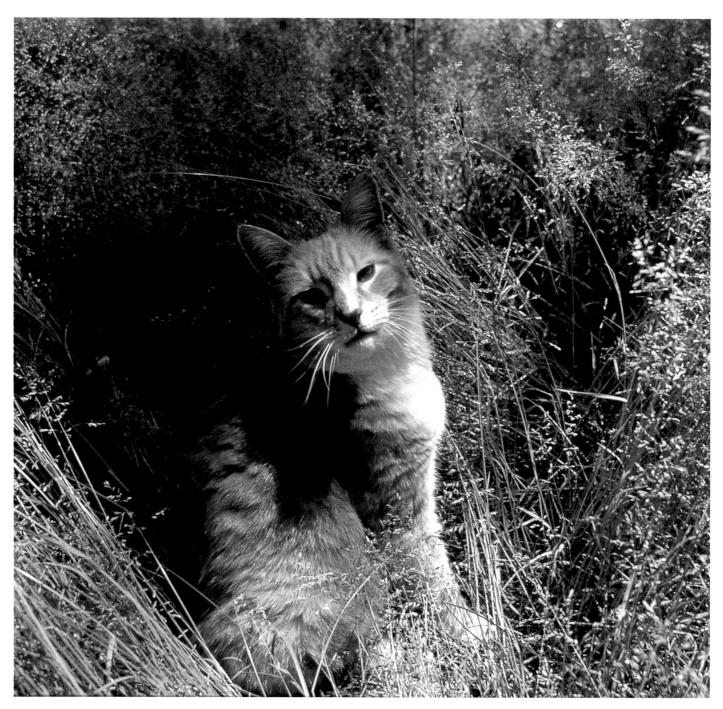

Some cats are natural stand outs.

cats for all seasons

Kitty gets blue.

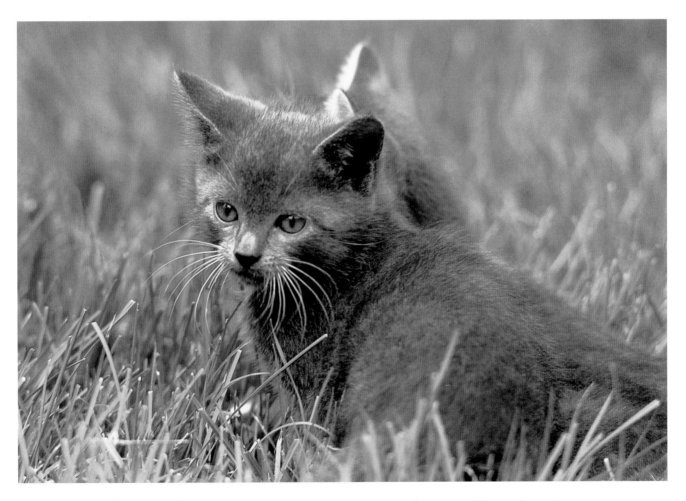

Patrolling the summer grass, kittens can rotate their ears and listen for voles.
A cat's hearing is five times better than our own in the higher ranges.

In the pink.

Flower power.

Plucked from obscurity.

Gateway to happiness.

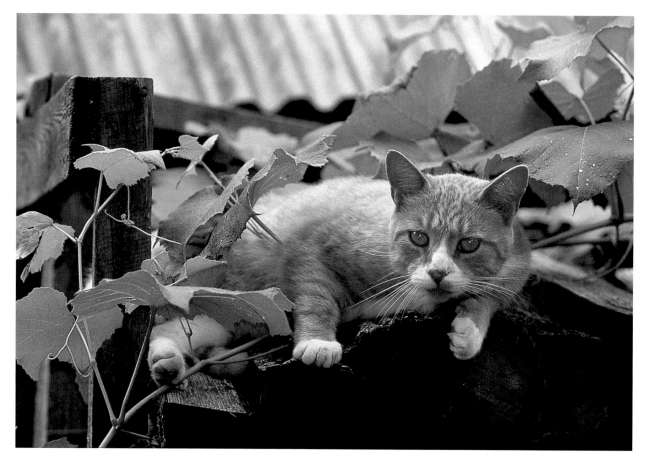

Ready to pounce (if absolutely necessary).

The lazy days of summer? Try exhausting.

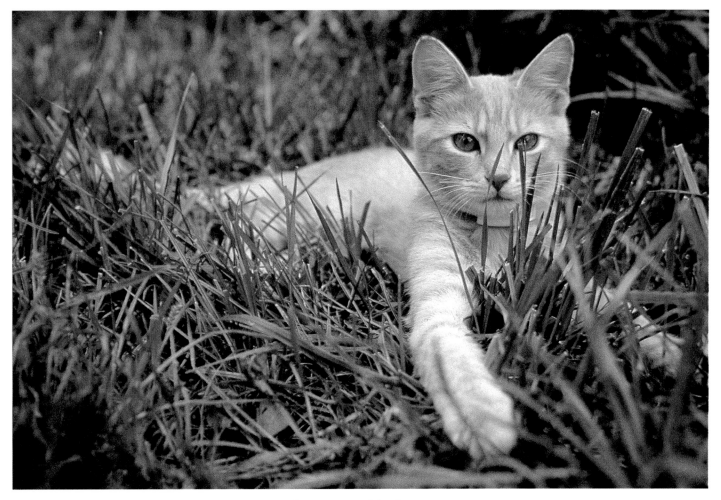

Long arm of the lawn.

The lazy days of summer.

cats for all seasons

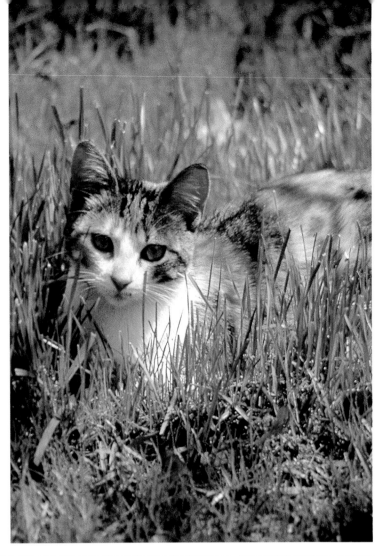

There's nothing like
the beginning of bug season.

Cats love to be secretive—
it's crucial to hunting in the wild.

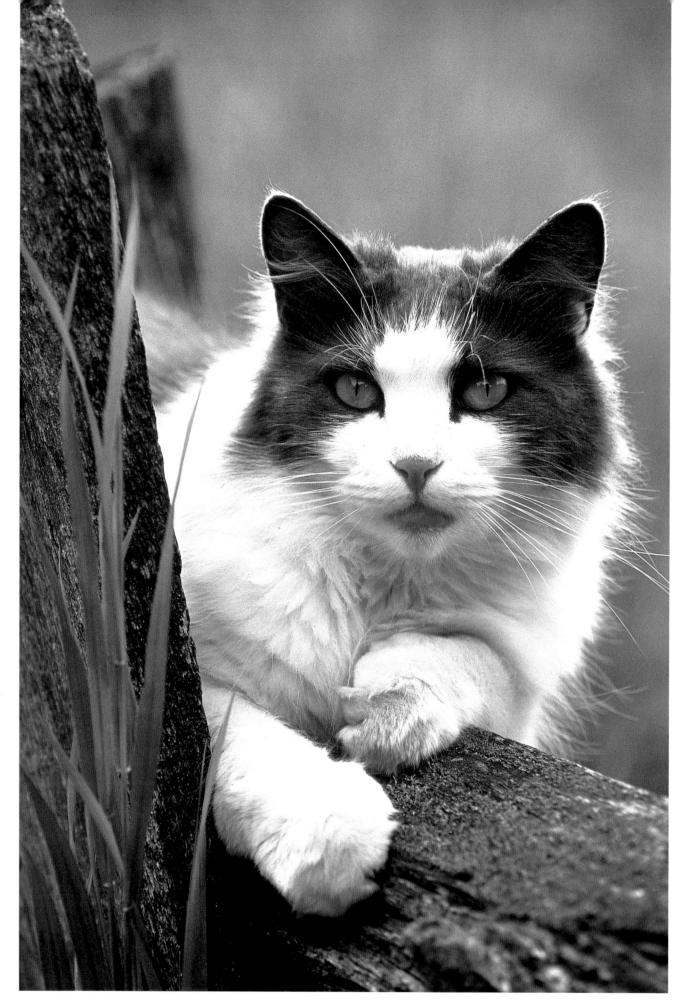

A little green always cheers me up.

cats for all seasons

To a cat, an empty tub is a good tub.

Not exactly puppy love.

A cat bouquet.

cats for all seasons

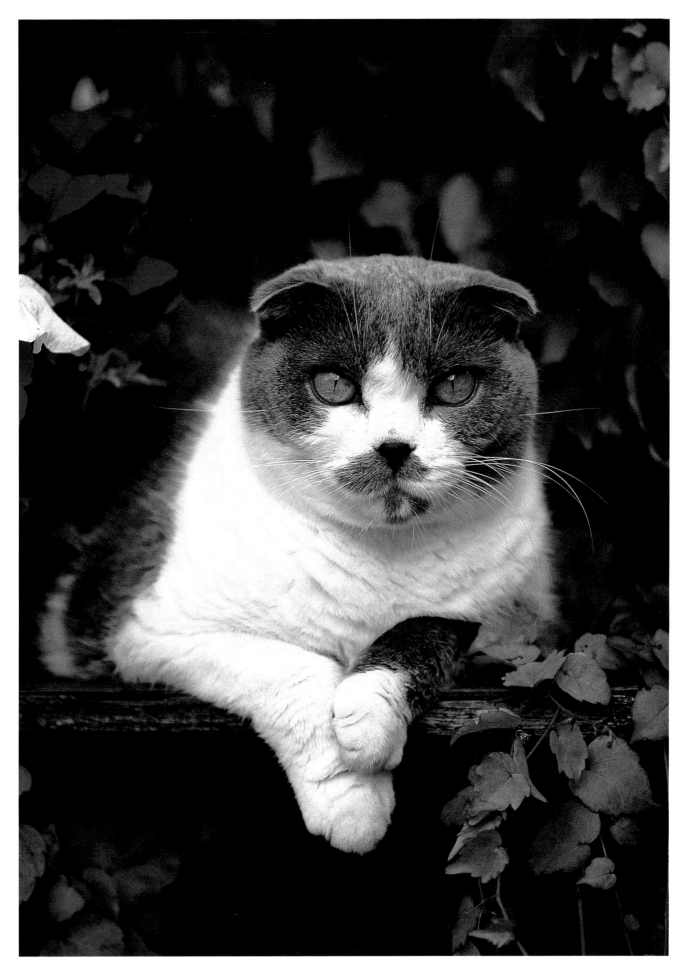

Portrait of a lady. The Scottish fold is noted for its sweet personality.

cats in action

One of the cat's most captivating traits is that it can make the transition from happy house cat to powerful predator in one graceful leap.

House cats around the world are capable of "going feral" with an effortless ease afforded no other domesticated species. We know the pretty puss propped up on velvet cushions is only steps away from becoming a little tiger out in the meadow. They have finely tuned senses of sight, hearing, and smell. They have the bodies of supreme athletes, and the instincts of skilled hunters.

Cats move through branches with startling agility. A complex inner ear helps establish balance and a rudder-like tail maintains it. Cats also have at their command a full arsenal of hunting moves. For catching mice there is a quick downward strike. For birds, an upward leap. And for fish there is a flip of the prey onto land. All of these gestures are used by kittens in play, which strengthens muscles and hones techniques.

But our cats do not have to ford streams and scale mountains for a brush with the wild. A ball of yarn or a shoelace can become wily prey that needs to be stalked and subdued. The best toys are light enough to move quickly when batted and soft enough to sink teeth into.

It seems our cats establish quirky patterns of play during kittenhood and often keep them long into adult years. Even our frumpy, dignified middle-aged cats will surprise us and engage in a youthful romp with a balled up piece of paper or a length of string from time to time. Many cats display "mad moments," when their napping ends quite suddenly and all the stored up energy fuels several minutes of crazy dashing around the apartment.

Though sometimes it can be quite distressing, our cats are efficient predators. Our two species first met up because of the cat's amazing ability to kill rodents. Now, however, we are often perplexed when our little companions bring home even smaller "companions"—a mouse, or worse still, half a mouse. How exact records are kept is anyone's guess, but books that keep tallies of such things often cite the world's best mousers, cats who are alleged to have dispatched tens of thousands of mice. Many of us would prefer that our cats work at ridding our apartments of balls of yarn.

First, check to see if the coast is clear. Next, it's a portal to a barn full of milk. . . .

cats in action

Suspended in time.

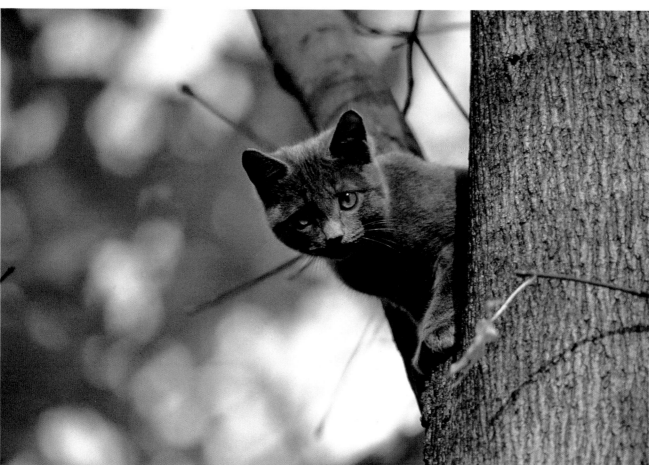

Barking up the wrong tree

Leaping a wide brook in a single bound.

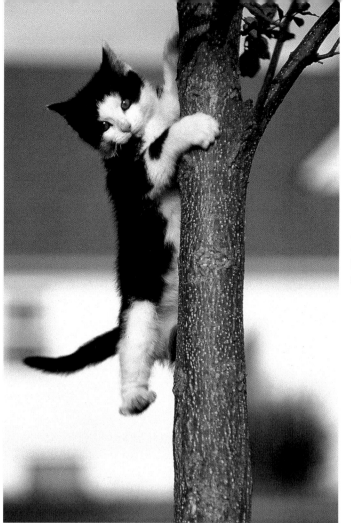

How is it that
going up was
so easy?

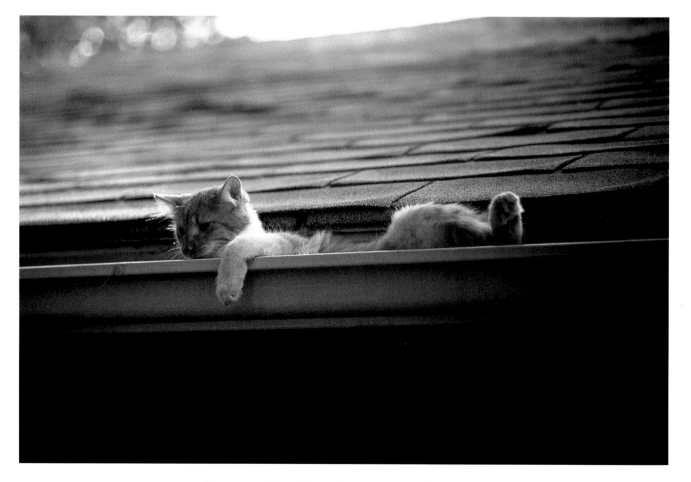

Some cats live life with one paw in the gutter.

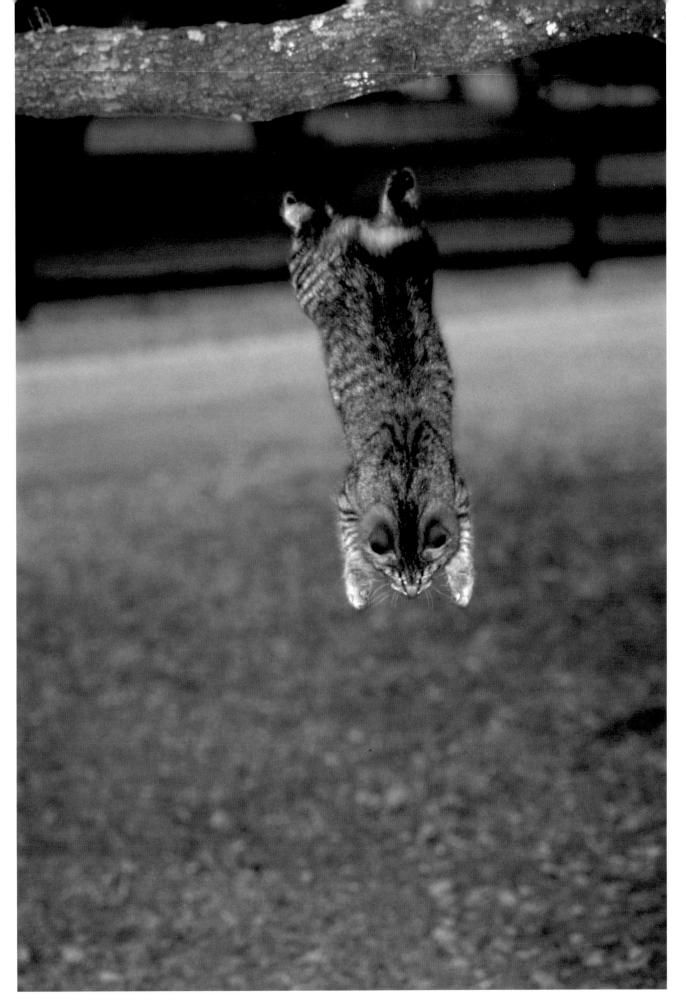

Feets, don't fail me now!

Branching out.

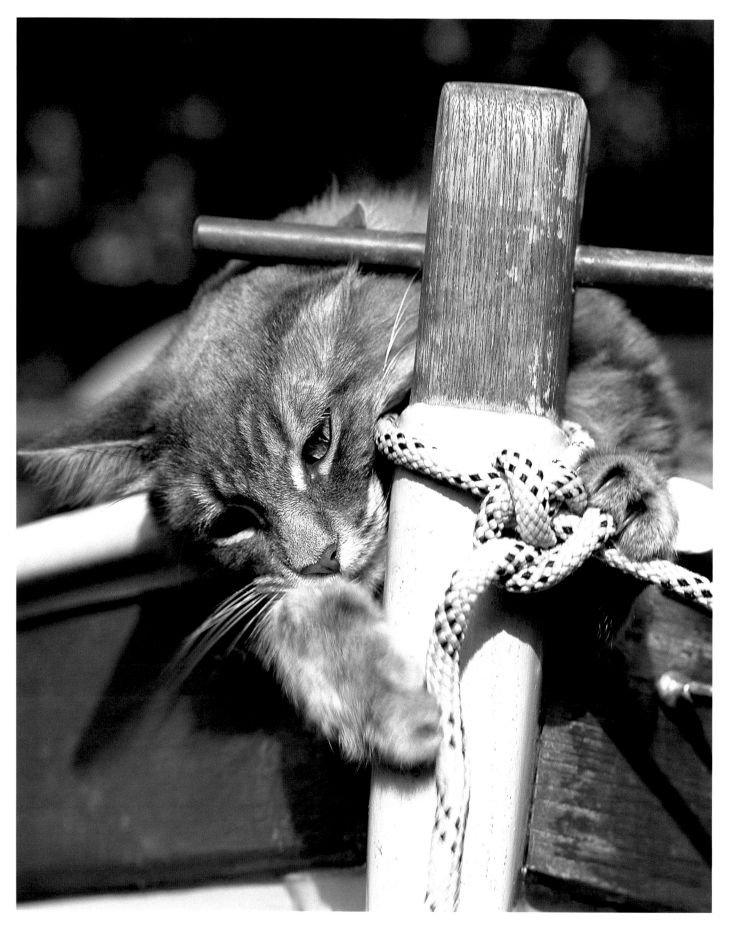

I'd rather be sailing.

cats in action

Drunk from too much twine.

Some cats prefer their laces al dente.

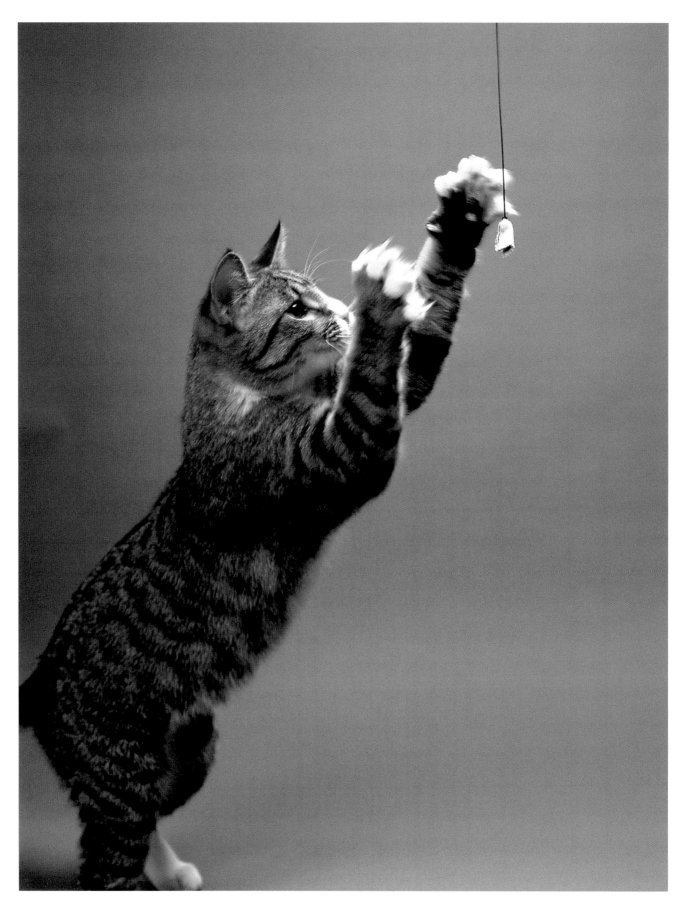

The stripes and the instincts of a tiger.

cats in action

Something to flip over.

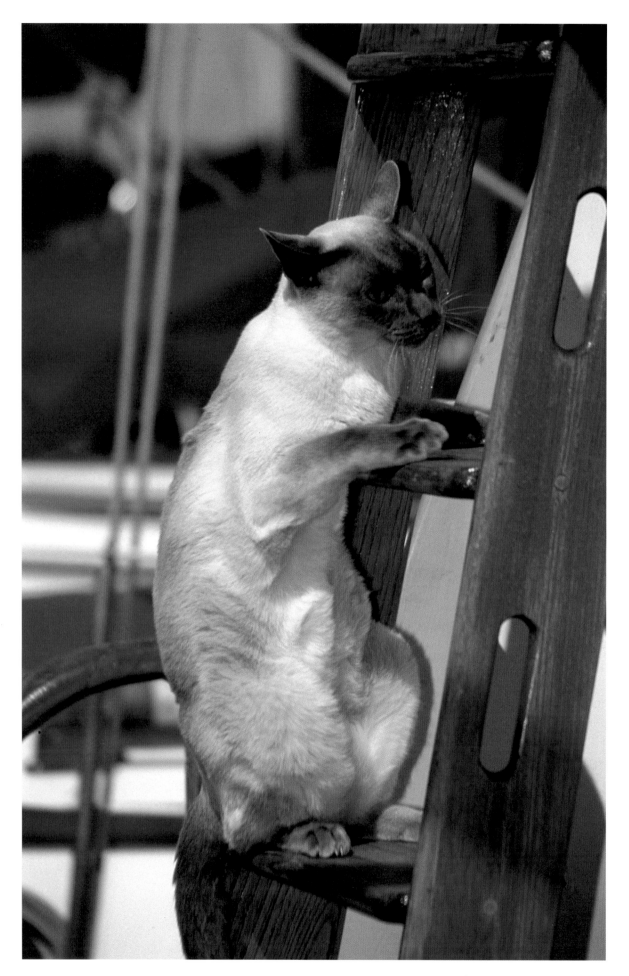

Climbing the ladder to success.

cats in action

kittens and cat-napping

It has been calculated that when a cat reaches nine years old, he or she has been awake for only three of them. (The three year figure is derived from the fact that the average house cat sleeps at least sixteen hours a day, twice that of the person lugging in the kitty litter and giant bags of food.)

That means six years of naps, sound sleeps, dozes, cat naps, and snoozes. Six years of nose twitches, paw flickers, and ear blinks. Six years of sunny spots and pillows and cushions. Six years of rest and relaxation.

Like other efficient predators, cats are built to nap between kills. And that can be a nice, long time. The experts have even broken catnapping down into two different categories — the light sleep, and the deep, solid slumber with its rapid eye movement and limb twitches.

Our feline companions don't go in for long periods of sleep like we do. They scatter theirs throughout a twenty-four-hour period, thus ensuring that they can be fully awake at the time we are in our soundest sleep.

In kittenhood and then again in old age, cats sleep more—up to eighty percent of the day. It's easy to see why kittens do this. Weighing about four ounces at birth, kittens double that in just the first week. Then there are two months of suckling and growing and eye openings and tooth eruptions. That's a lot work.

But it seems the work of cats is to sleep anyway. Part of what we enjoy in cats is the sense of peace we feel when we see a contented cat curled up or stretched out in blissful slumber. The body is limp and the attitude is relaxed. When a wary predator such as our cat is asleep, it means no harm is near. There is nothing to fear. We relax, too.

Do cats dream? Scientists say brain wave activity during their deep sleep is similar to our own in that stage, but we cannot really tell if cats experience dreams the way we do. The only way we'll be sure is if our cats learn to talk. But then, do we really want them stumbling downstairs in the morning in their little cat pajamas and boring us at the breakfast table with half remembered dreams the way friends do? "I was running through the backyard, chasing a mouse, well, it wasn't really a mouse . . . ."

A sleeping cat tells us all is right with the world. It brings us peace and tranquillity. And once you have shared your life with a cat, a pool of warm sunlight splashed across the floor just looks empty without a sweet cat dozing in it.

Singing the praises of sleep.

Dreamy eyes. A cat's eyes tell us a lot about mood. When the eyes are open wide,
the cat is alert; when the eyes are half-closed, the cat is relaxed and trusting.

kittens and cat-napping

Cat's cradle.

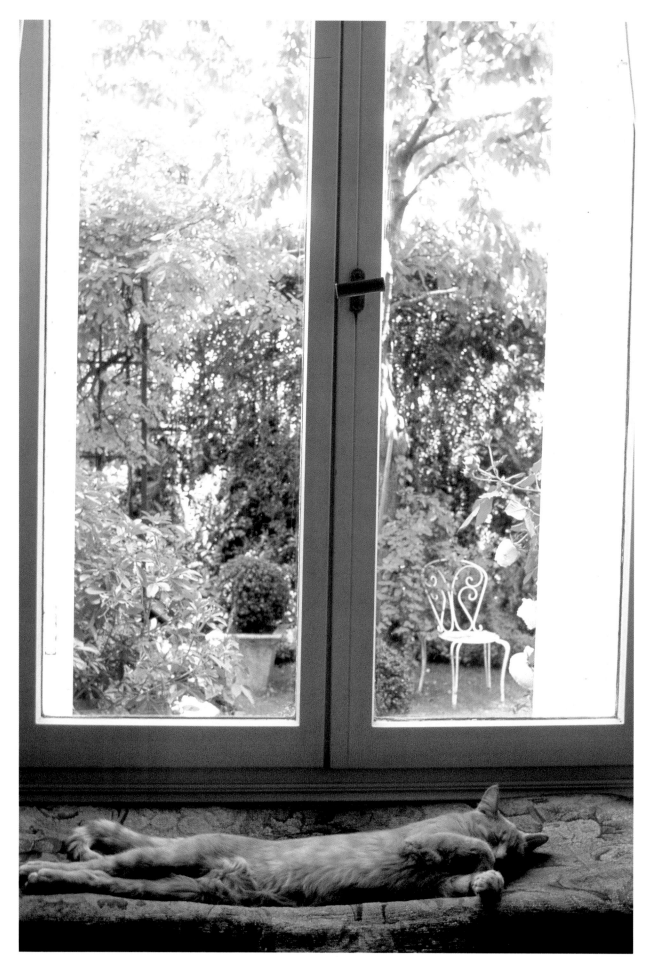

Garden of the feline-Continis.

kittens and cat-napping

Now blanket coverage.

Swept away.

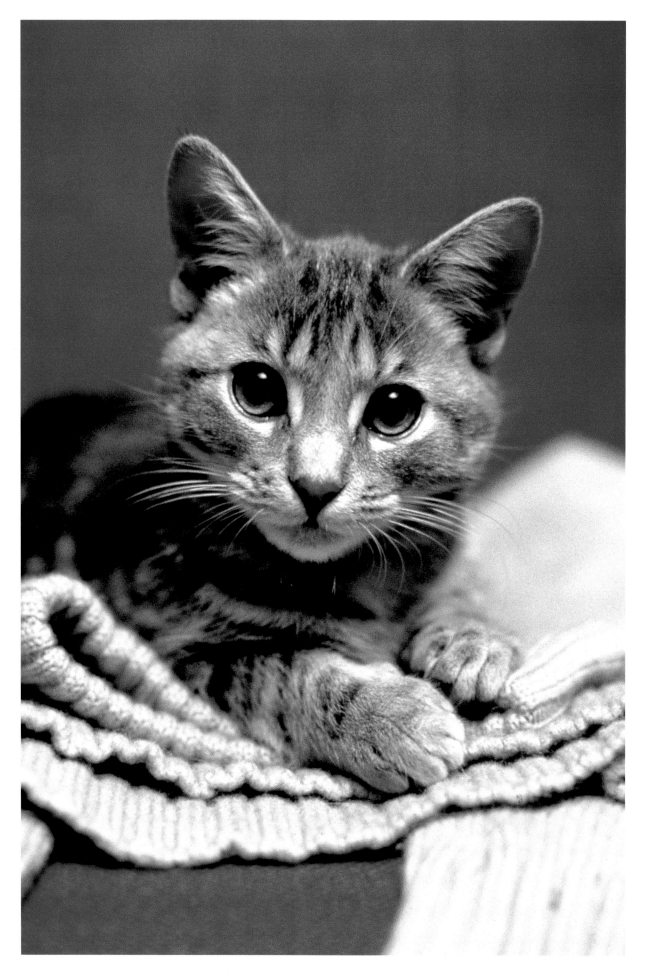

Please, do not disturb.

kittens and cat-napping

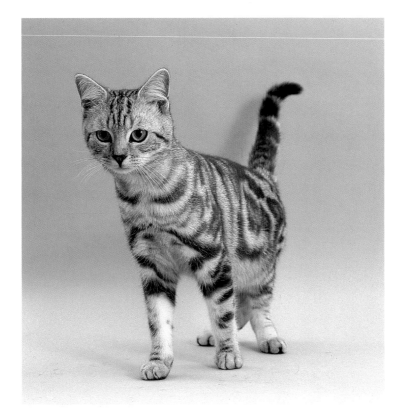

Black and white and fur all over.

Who needs a scratching post?

It's not comfortable, but it will do.

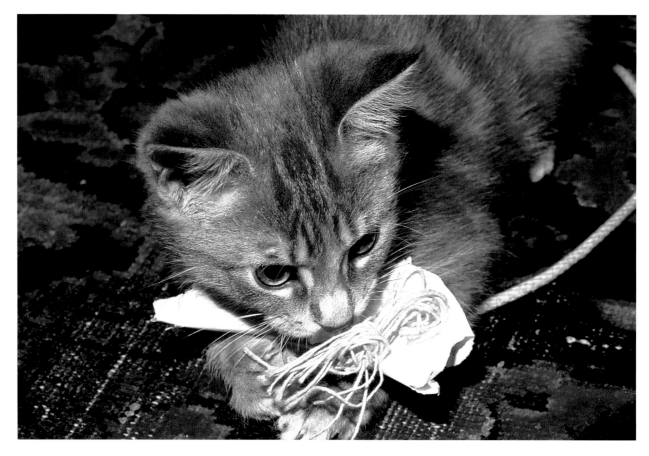

After a snooze, she's got the world on a string.

Not a creature was stirring.

The hidden life of cats.

Turn out the lights already!

Taking a nap on the wild side.

kittens and cat-napping

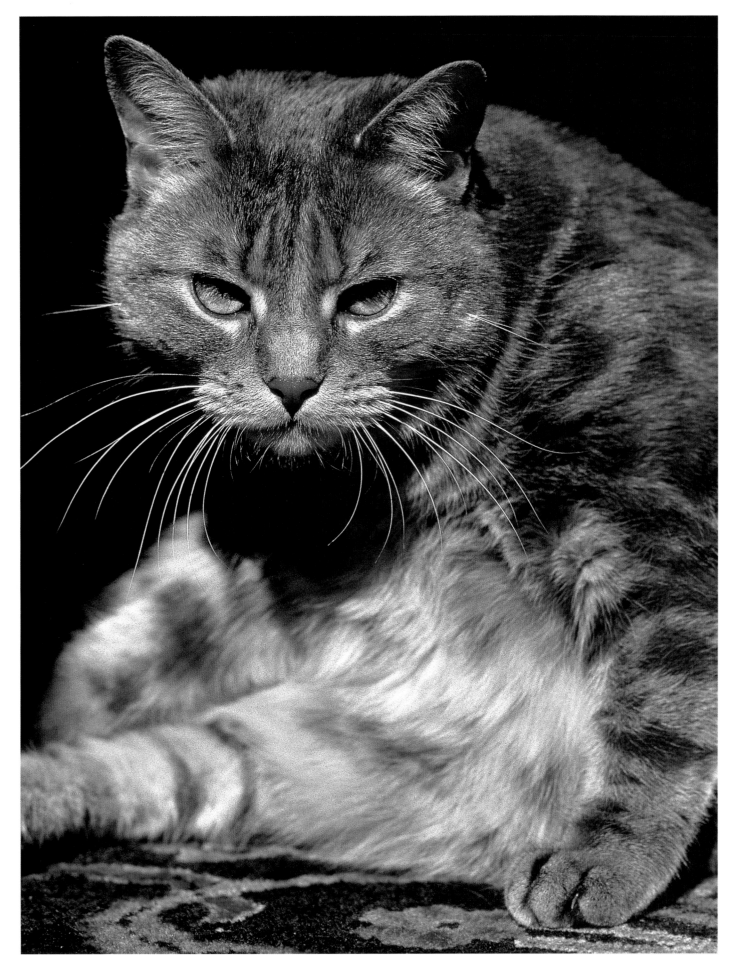

Sometimes it is also best to let sleeping **cats** lie.

kittens and cat-napping

the well-traveled cat

It is hard to imagine as we struggle to get our cats into carriers or into cars that they have such a well-traveled heritage. "I couldn't survive a two-block ride in the station wagon," they yowl. "How cruel to wrench me from hearth and home!" they scream. And yet not so many generations ago, our cats were navigating the uncharted seas, enjoying the life of the salty vagabond.

As soon as ships were used for trade, there wasn't one at sea that could hold down the healthy on-board rat population without a few ocean-going tabbies. Sailors valued their high seas mousers for keeping their stores of food safe, or at least much safer. That could be a matter of life or death on long voyages. To the crew, cats were heroes. And to the cats, the journey must have seemed like a vacation cruise—life was a constant banquet with plentiful food ready and warm. Rats on a raft, what could be better?

Felines today may have given up their seafaring ways in large part, but as we travel we get to see cats in exotic surroundings. They really don't appear any different the world over. (So how is it that in Paris even a scruffy calico can seem so . . . soignée? Maybe it's in the accented "miaou.")

Wherever in the world we find them, cats always look singularly at home. The country cat, so fit and robust, hunting the meadow, overseeing the work in the barn—that's perfection. The city cat, so self-possessed and sleek. This cat enjoys the nightlife—the lights along the skyline, the sounds of jazz in the air. And by day, there is so much to watch in the streets below, so much gossip to collect. This seems awfully perfect, too.

And who could be better placed than the lucky cat close to the water? Whether by fresh or salt water, there will always be plenty of fish. The portrait of this cat is also just right.

What we do know is that many cats have difficulty traveling or moving beyond their primary stomping ground. Are they sensitive to magnetic forces? Or are they just loathe to surrender any hard-won coziness?

A cat can kayak without ever touching an oar.

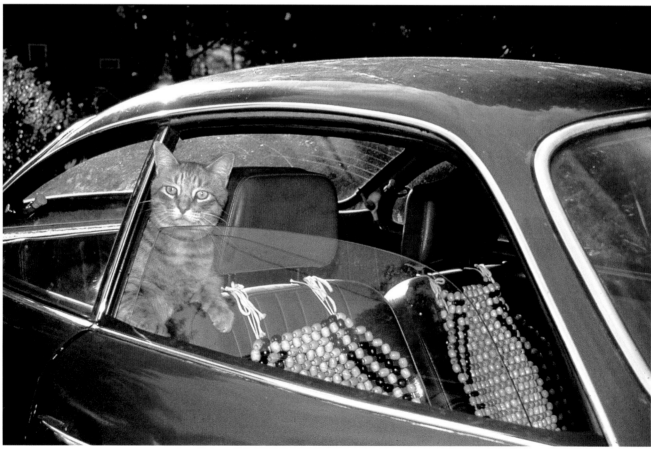

Backseat driver.

the well-traveled cat

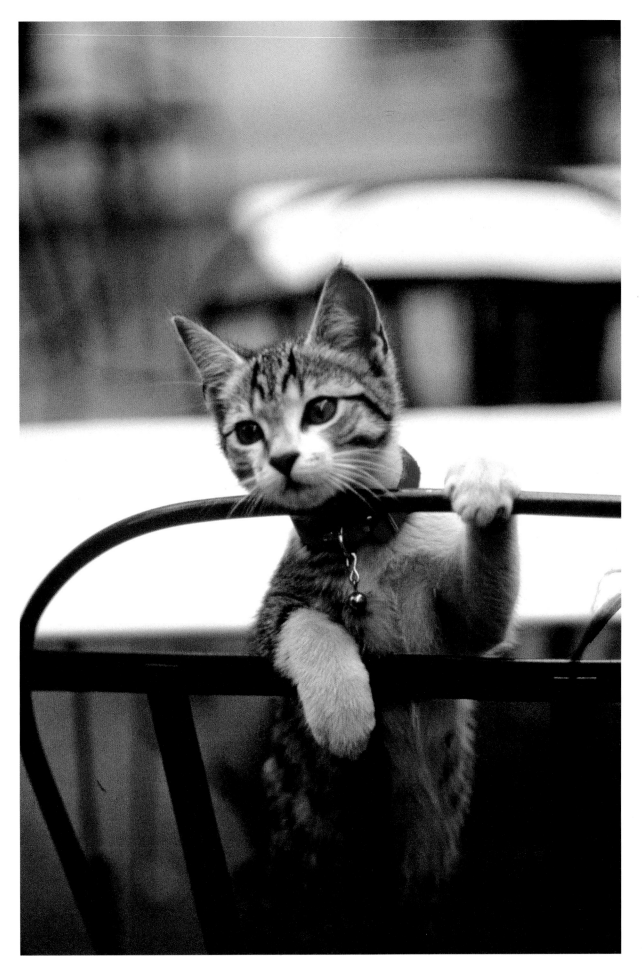

There's always so much to see.

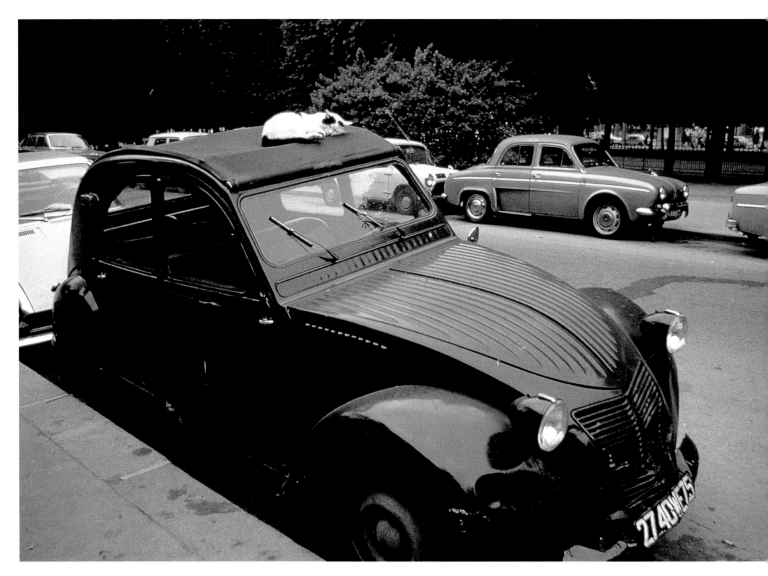

Wake me up before you go.

Keep on truckin'.

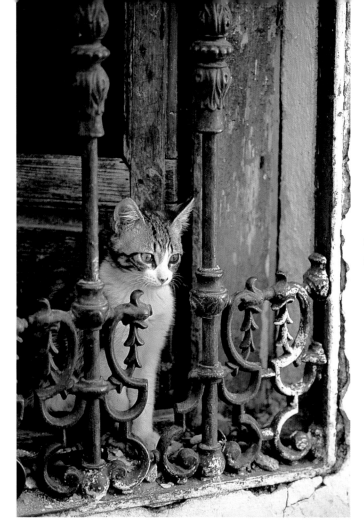

Oh, my . . .
sardine truck at six o'clock.

I'm ready for my close-up, Mr. DeMew.

the well-traveled cat

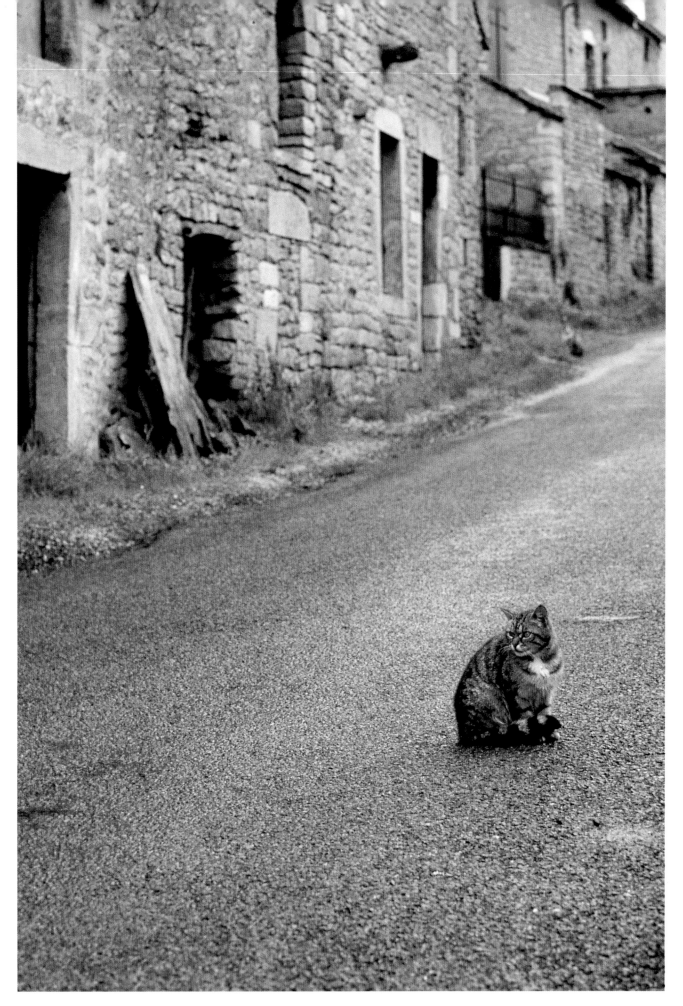

Taking the high road. Rudyard Kipling wrote of the independent nature of cats
in "The Cat That Walked by Himself."

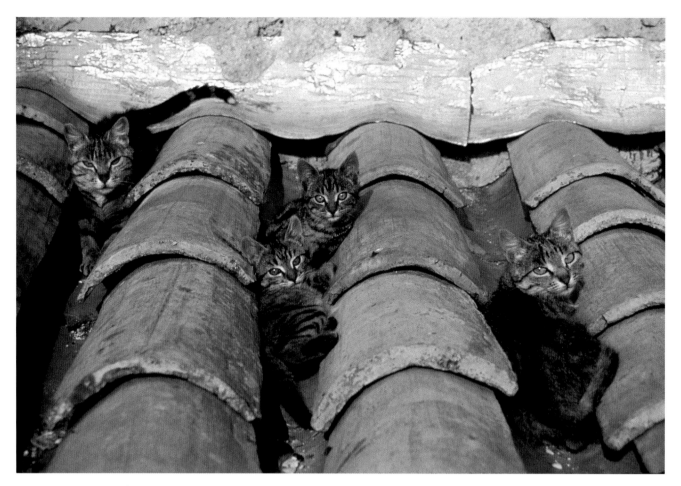

Cats on a hot terra-cotta roof.

You'll never guess who I bumped into today.

the well-traveled cat

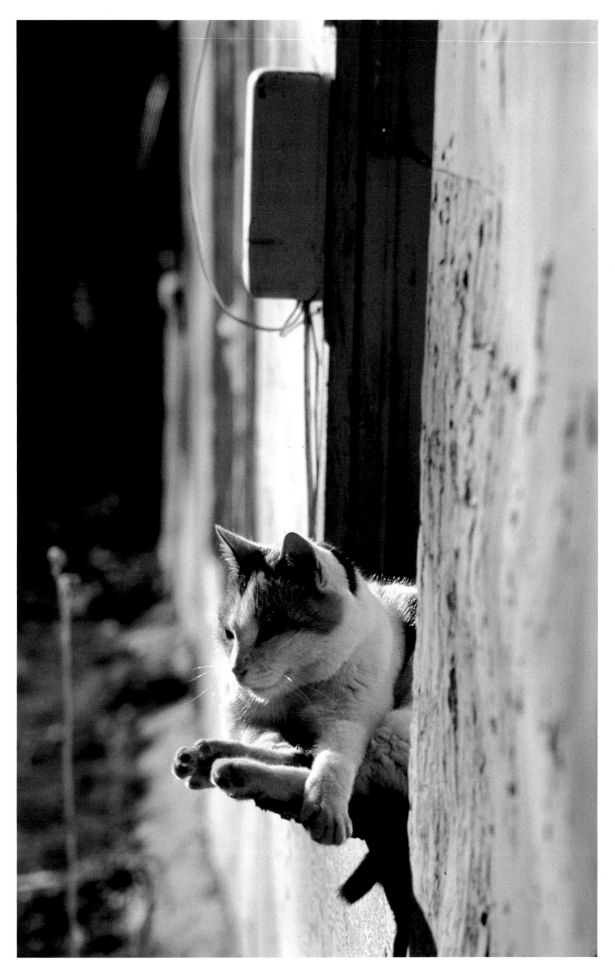

Narrow, yes, but it will do.

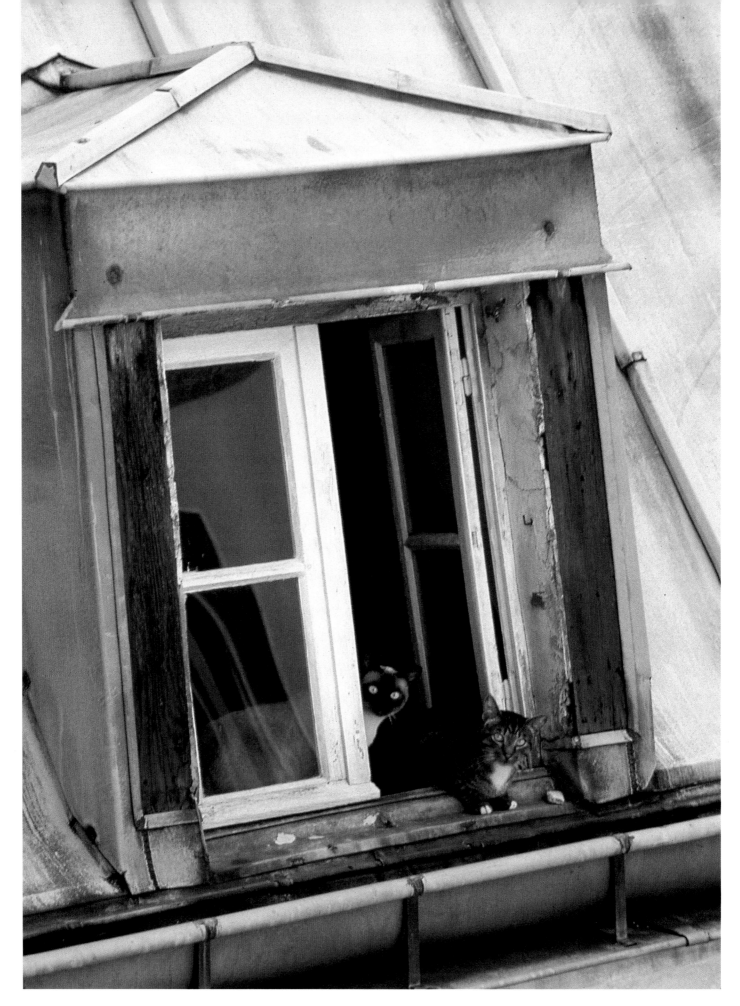

Looks like rain to me.

the well-traveled cat

Born to be mild.

The bars keep dogs out. They do not keep cats in.
I just happen to like it here.

the well-traveled cat

Feline cityscape.

Cafe society.

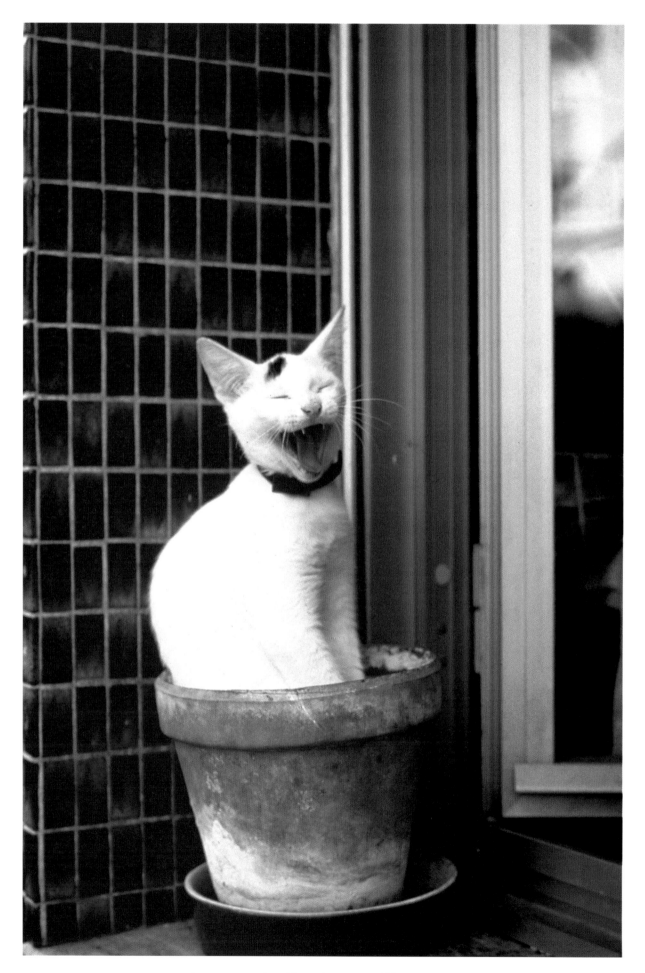

A meow with a French accent. This potted
cat calls Nice, France, home.

the well-traveled cat

Any family resemblance? Like their wild and distant relatives, cats know how to take care of themselves.

The ladies who bench.

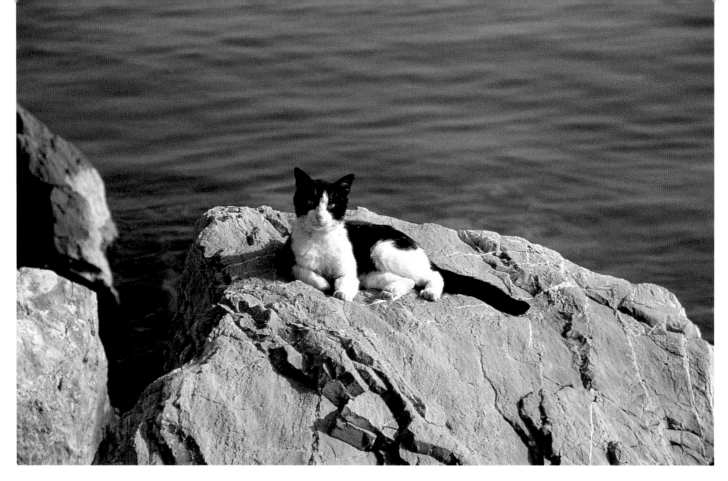

The weather is beautiful, and so am I.

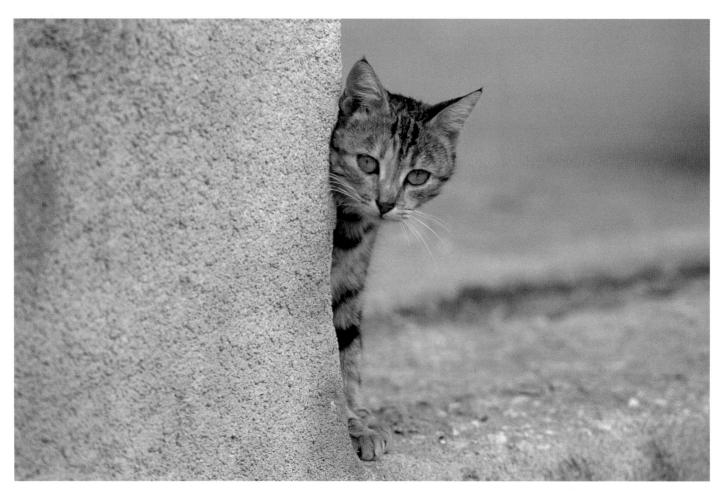

Uh-oh, here comes Rover and his gang

Cats in the belfry.

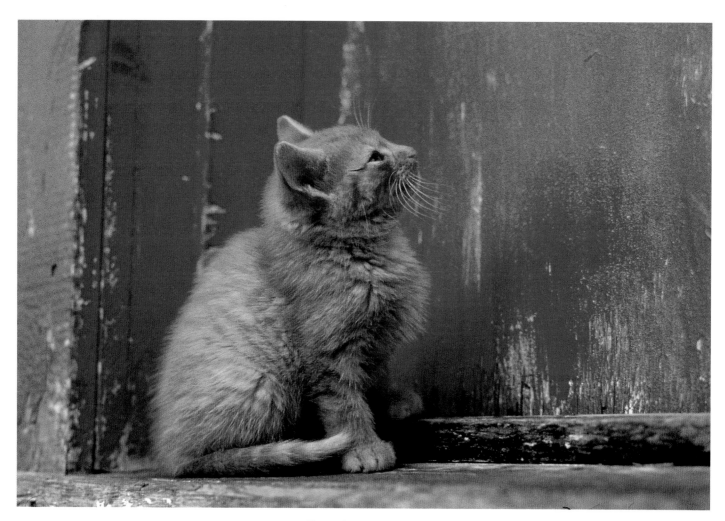

Paint the town red.

A place to be seen.

A simple, garden-variety cat.

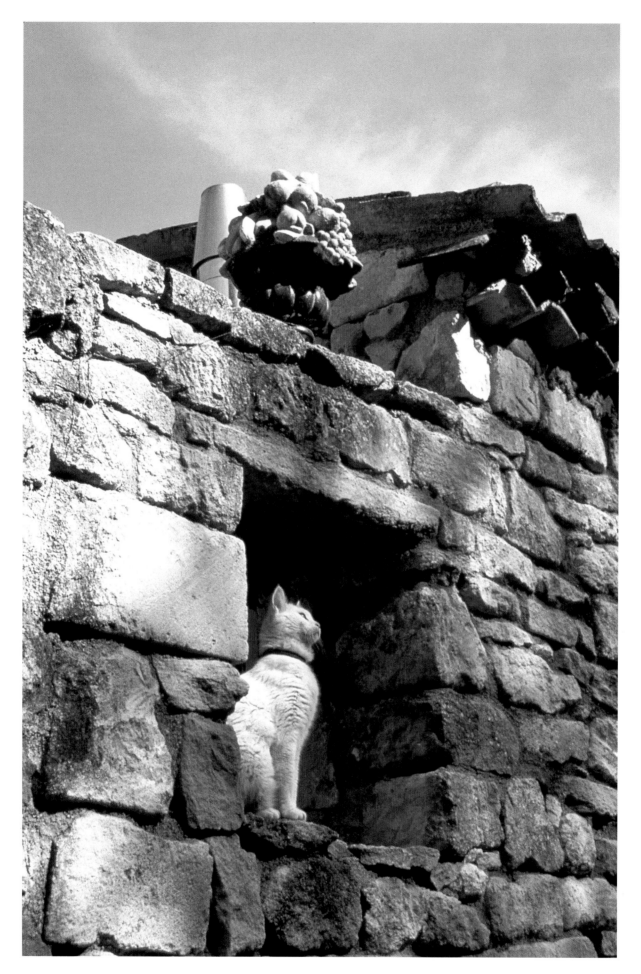

Sentry cat

the well-traveled cat

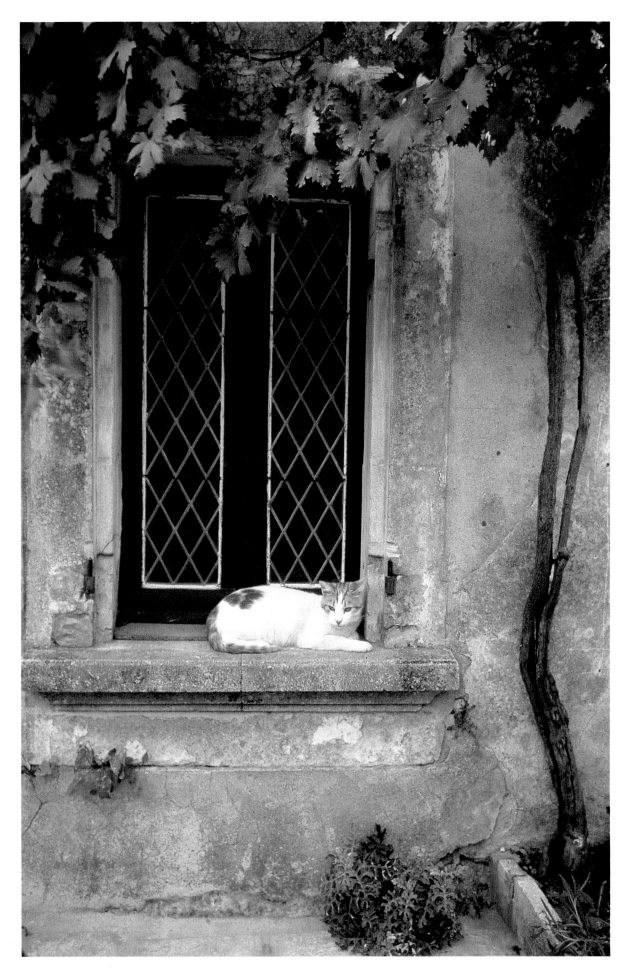

My sill is my castle.

Palatial digs.

the well-traveled cat

Reflections of feline beauty.

Two cats with the blues.

The peace of a park bench.

Ah, village life.

Steppin' out.

Bewitching, no?

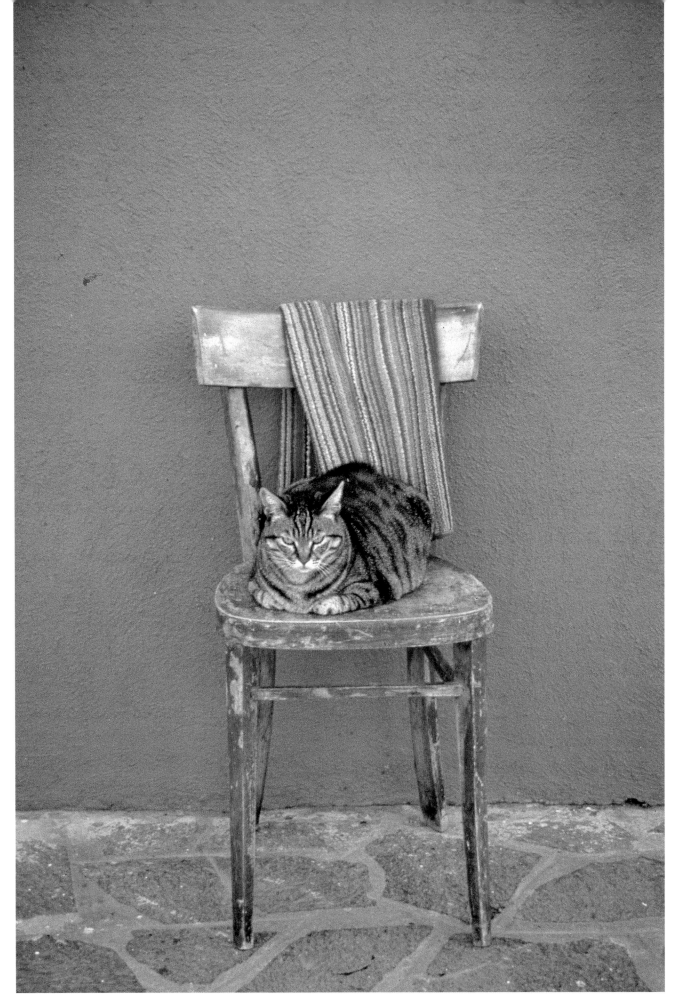

Chairman of the bored.

the well-traveled cat

Cathedral cat.

A step up on the social ladder.

the industrious cat

Cats and work?

The two must seem antithetical to those of us acting as the humble servants to a feline. But believe it or not, cats had a big job to do when they first began their association with us. And since then we have been employing them in all kinds of places. Unlike dogs, who have been bred to hunt or herd or guard, our cats usually have one mission: kill rodents. This skill has made cats invaluable to Egyptian farmers, hungry sailors, and to book lovers and postal clerks alike.

Wherever we have been victimized by nibbling vermin, we have been saved by pouncing, predatory cats. Hard-working cats have kept valuable tomes safe in libraries around the world. For in a library the cat is the perfect solution to a nasty problem. They keep mice from destroying valuable manuscripts, and they do it quietly. For more than a century, cats have been keeping England's post offices (a place filled with food parcels and paper) from being overrun by vermin. Cats have even helped various war efforts by killing rats aboard battleships.

In the world of high-stakes horse racing, cats have more than proved their worth as stablemates. There are famous stories that date from the 1700s about great racers who were wildly attached to feline companions. The 1945 Kentucky Derby winner, Daunt, was supposed to have shared a great bond with a tom named Ginger.

But while we think of the work of cats as being so singular in focus, there is another job they've moved into with absolute feline ease: stress reduction. Out of the barn and into our homes, one of the biggest jobs for cats today is keeping us happy and healthy. It is known, for example, that pets can lower our blood pressure and help us recover faster from injury or illness.

It is the job of the cat in modern society to meet us at the door and invite a greeting session. To sit on our laps on lazy days and purr. To keep us honest by never being impressed by our professional accomplishments. And to give us the same look whether we've just woken up with a bad case of "bedhead" or if we've just dressed for an evening out. They are accomplished stablemates and soul mates.

We find them around the world, in all kinds of situations, but whatever job our cats take on, and wherever they do it, they pull it off with élan.

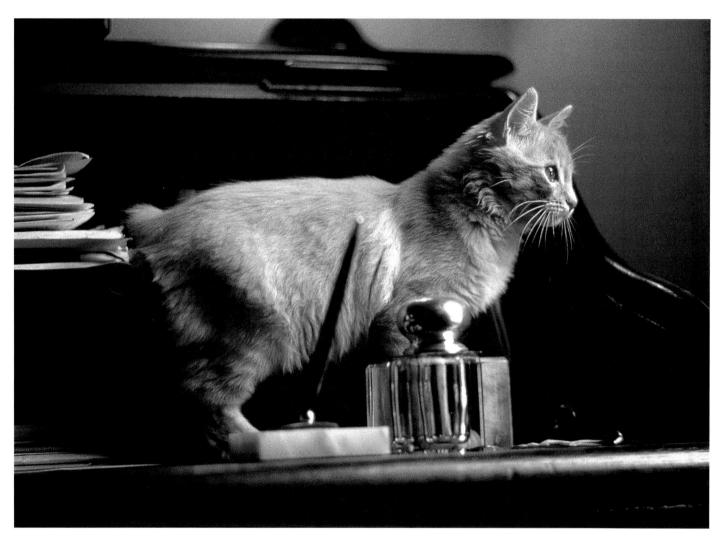

A kitten with the write stuff.

the industrious cat

The very definition of a cat. Throughout history, libraries have employed cats to keep valuable books safe from marauding mice.

Siamese motto: Buy low, sell high.

Whiskers Fresno Firecracker Ampersand Circe Bozo Madeline Duchess Checkers
Norman Godzilla Hercules Shortstuff Dandelion Tigger Cyrano Abner Cupcake
Fuzzy Face Sylvester Bandit Rosaline Zeus Inkspot Slate Nova Nougat Jason
Ebony Venus Jingles Pandora Twinkle Toes Elvis Carlyle Sugar Camille Utah
Mickey Emily Anthracite Solo Saturn Chocolate Monty Kumquat Eggnog Quark
Cinderella Valentine Corkscrew Fireworks Princess Bruno Aurora Microchip
Tornado Marcus Juliet Kni ht Margo Phoenix Fluffy Socks Freedom Scorpio
Pica Falstaff Rambo   lf Pint Nemo Nimbus Samson Pearl Rocky Picnic
Rufus Sherlock Clec   ilver Tina Summer Midnight Hyphen Precious
Karma Othell   copia Winston Lucky Friday Neko Felix
Sweetheart Pu   aract Bodoni Nigel Bastet Max Cottontail
Deputy Orson   w Harley Prancer Goblin Galahad Kiko Dawn
Merlin Bill   pokes Francois Butch Zelda King Professor
Orbit Satin   mmetry Foxy Lady Mitzy Cody Asia Zachary
Captain Anna   on Syrup Punky Rudolf July Senator Mary
Kaleidosco   e Candy Morrison Bonnie Piglet Pickles
Jake Velv   rts Faith Moe Jewel Fransisco Ace Fiend
Pee Wee Ba   ntas Fritz Voodoo Ohm Sigmund Harmony Karl
Spot Harmonica   George Sir Stomper Ruth Fisher Jones Romeo Babs
Muffin Casey Bobo Vincent Thomas Furball Ralph Doc Bugs Justice Como Chopper
Whiskers Fresno Firecracker Ampersand Circe Bozo Madeline Duchess Checkers
Norman Godzilla Hercules Shortstuff Dandelion Tigger Cyrano Abner Cupcake
Fuzzy Face Sylvester Bandit Rosaline Zeus Inkspot Slate Nova Nougat Jason
Ebony Venus Jingles Pandora Twinkle Toes Elvis Carlyle Sugar Camille Utah
Mickey Emily Anthracite Solo Saturn Chocolate Monty Kumquat Eggnog Quark
Cinderella Valentine Corkscrew Fireworks Princess Bruno Aurora Microchip
Tornado Marcus Juliet Knight Margo Phoenix Fluffy Socks Freedom Scorpio
Pica Falstaff Rambo Sandy Half Pint Nemo Nimbus Samson Pearl Rocky Picnic
Rufus Sherlock Cleopatra Quicksilver Tina Summer Midnight Hyphen Precious
Karma Othello Muff Lenora Hero Cornucopia Winston Lucky Friday Neko Felix

Reading between the lines.

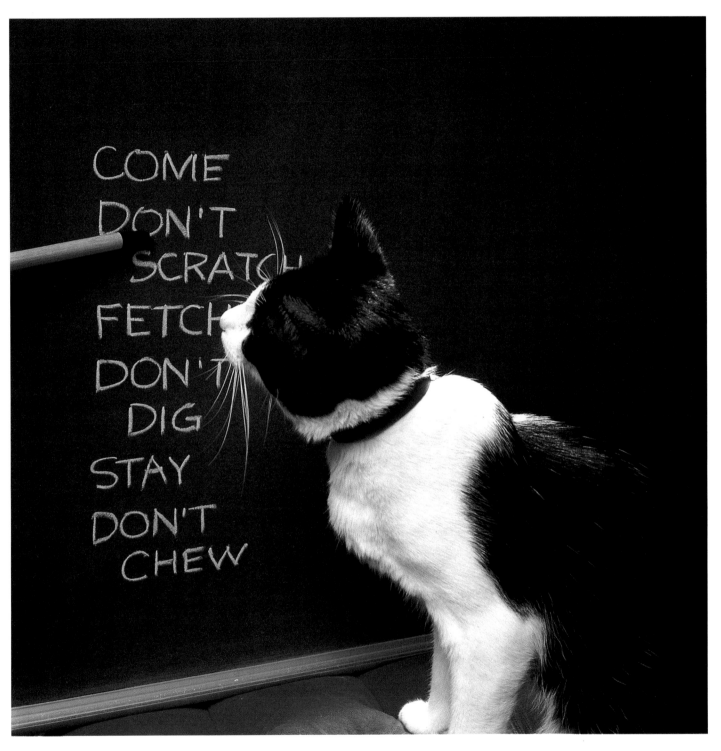

Do I have to spell it out for you?

Some cats give their all for art.

What's this about
"man's best friend"?

Drumming up business.

Preparing for Halloween.

Basking in the glow of the fall sun.

the industrious cat

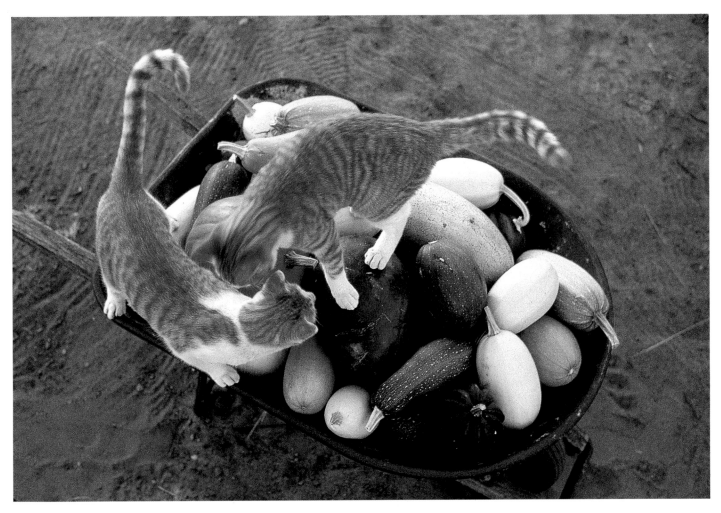

Are you out of your gourd?

Some prefer the honest labor of life in the country.

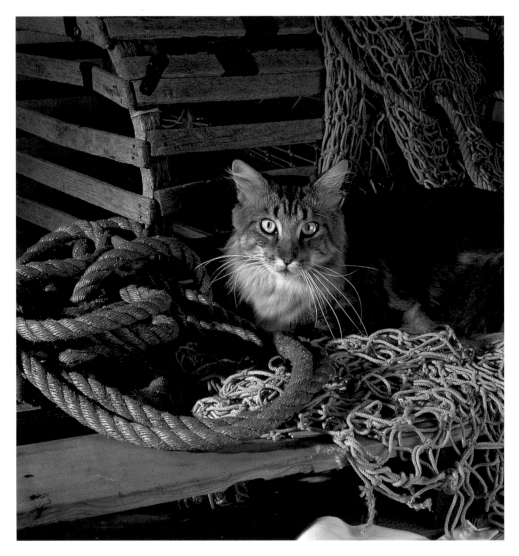

Others enjoy the rugged seafaring life.

the industrious cat

And still others take time out to pursue the good life.

cats & company

If cats could befriend such a strange species as ours, why should we be surprised when we find them cuddled up with dogs or rabbits or lambs?

For all their fabled aloofness, our cats turn out to be quite warm and friendly. Selective, yes, always selective, but that does not preclude affection. And it makes it all the more meaningful when they do choose to spend some precious time with us.

Cats are able to give and receive what we very well might call love with an array of unlikely partners. That's not so complicated really. But the trouble with us humans is that we don't always recognize friendly signals in cats. They're subtle, and we don't always do well with subtlety. We often need to be hit over the head with affection (if that's physically possible).

Cats do not bowl us over with attachment the way dogs do, jumping and nudging. But notice that our cats so often stay close to us in a quiet and low-key way. They notice where we're going and they magically show up in the same room. They always happen to be precisely in the area where we are. A dog will follow you noisily from room to room, but a cat will shadow you without tipping his . . . paw.

They are, in fact, signaling sociability, but we don't always get it. Other animals, however, seem to pick up on the signs. The scenes are unmistakable: dire enemies—the cat and dog—curled up together on a sofa in a long, drawn-out grooming session. They have no trouble translating each other's body language. When a Great Dane "grooms" a little cat with a big wet lap, it may seem a bit coarse to the cat, but she puts up with it. Patience, hardly every attributed to cats, really does exist in those feline souls.

How many of us have seen our cats have to contend with a new puppy in the house? They may not be happy about it, they may stay at higher elevations for a while, but eventually they seem to teach these large, bold, young things the rules of the household.

And out in the barn, chickens and roosters may kick up more curiosity than affection in cats, but cows and horses often get the full kitty love treatment. And if a cow wanted to repay some of that feline friendliness with a little milk? Well, that would be fine, too.

Whether snoozing with a schnauzer or purring in our laps or even staring down barnyard fowl, it's clear our "solitary" cats love company.

Not a whiff of conflict.

An uneasy peace.

You are my sunshine.

Love tap.

And they said it wouldn't
work out. Though cats
and dogs are supposed to
be bitter enemies, many
live in absolute tranquillity.

Don't call my mother a dog.

He's not the kind of cat some girls think of as handsome,
but he carries the key to my heart.

cats & company

A different game of cat and mouse.

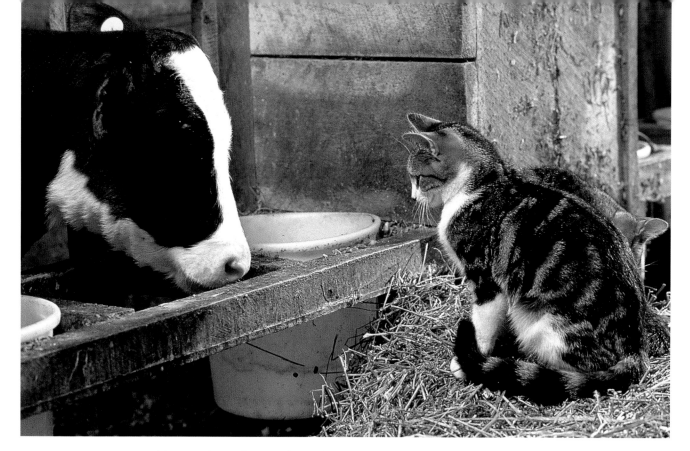

I know the milk is in there, I just don't know how to get it out.
(Milk can actually upset the stomachs of many adult cats who are lactose intolerant.)

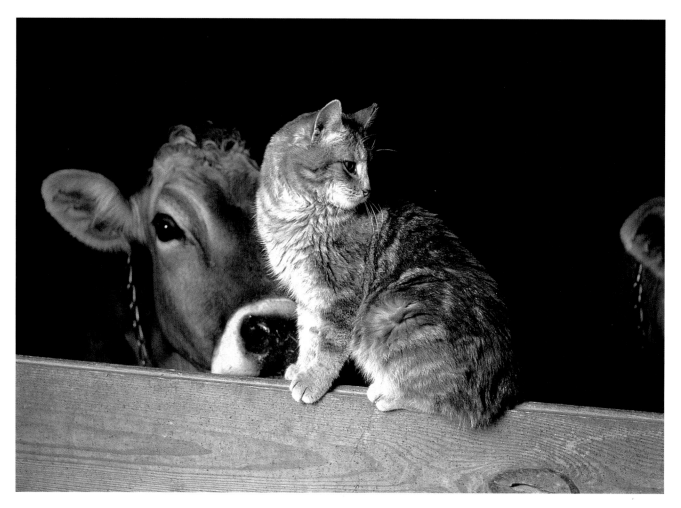

The cream of the crop.

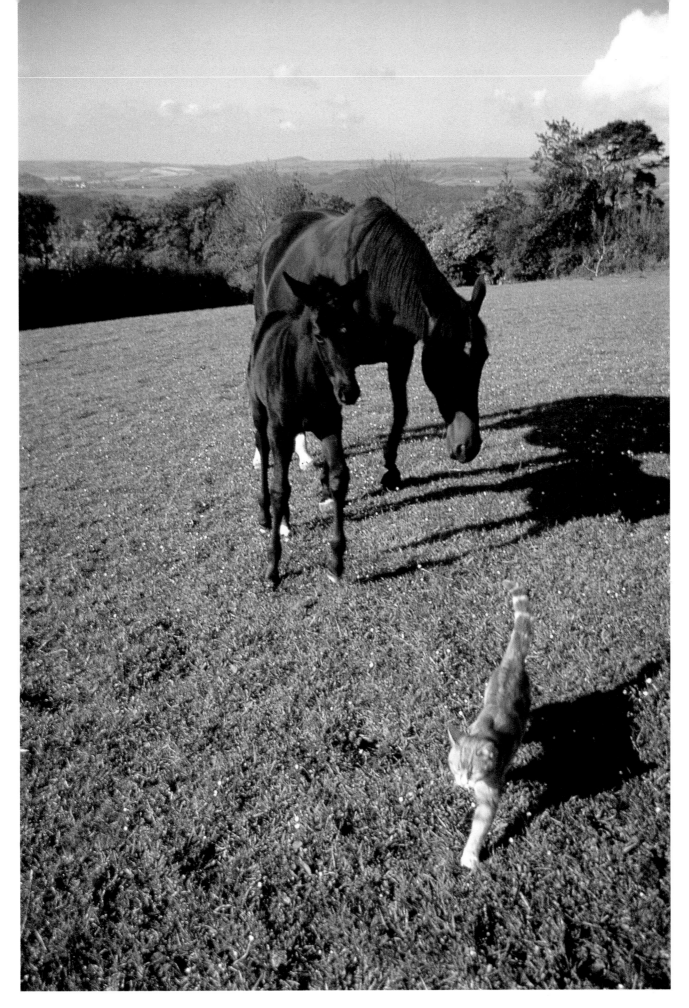

All creatures great and small.

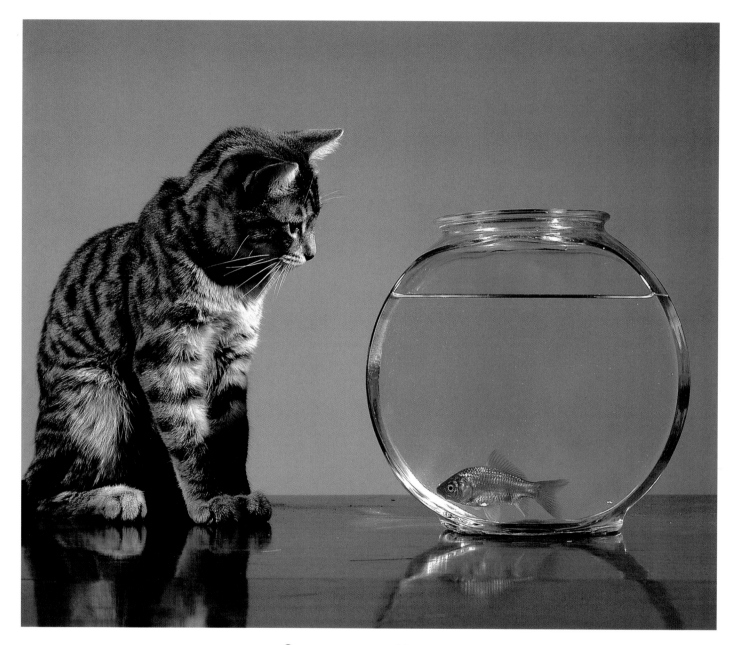

Cats are renowned hunters,
and one of their most important weapons is patience.

cats & company

Really, I just want to be friends, come on out.
Movement triggers an instinctive hunting response in cats.

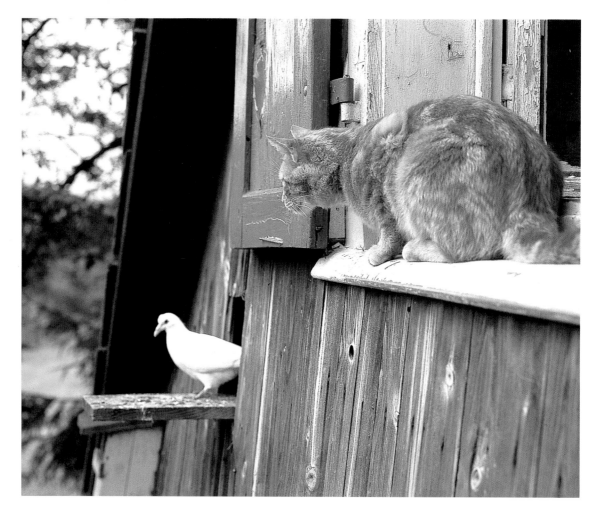

Watch the birdie . . . .

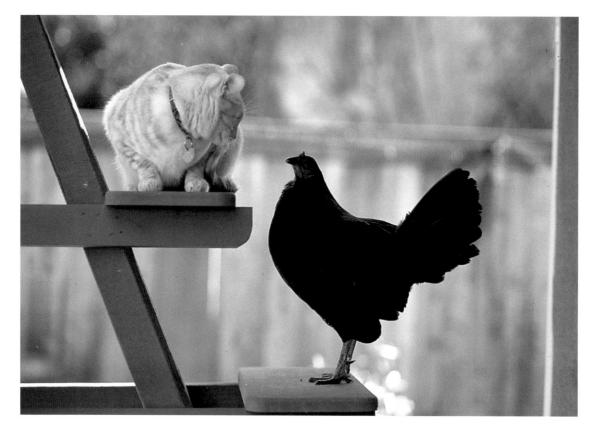

Evolutionary ladder?

cats & company

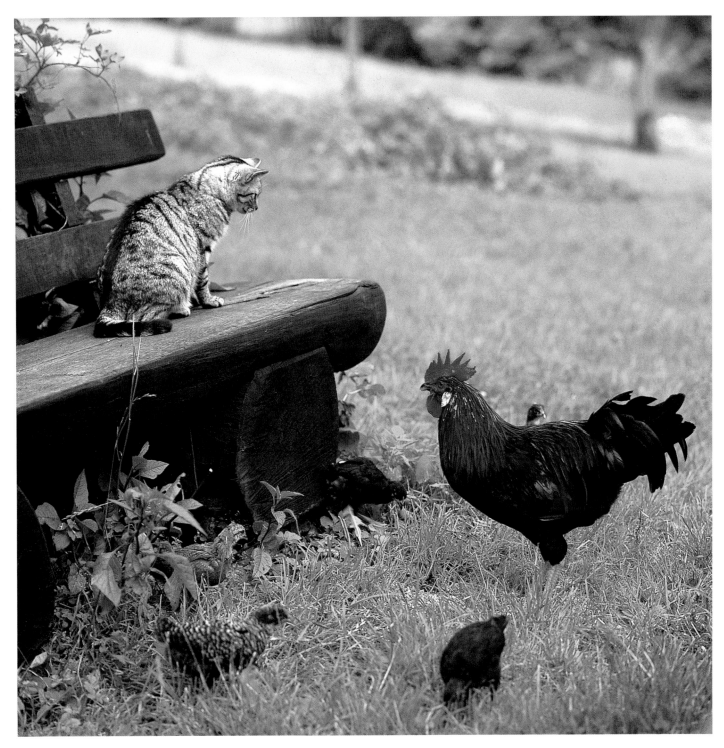

Don't mess with my girls.

Photography Credits

Credits are listed alphabetically by photographer.

© Jordana Abrams, New York: 10–11; © B & C Alexander, Dorset, U.K.: 25 top, 107; © Barbara Alper/Tom Keller & Associates, New York: front cover, 83 top; © Dimitry Baranov/Tom Keller & Associates, New York: 105 top; © Norvia Behling, St. Germain, Wis.: 40, 59, 132, 134 top; © J. Bisley/Unicorn Stock Photos, Kansas City, Mo.: 43; © Cheryl Blair, Worthington, Ohio: 53 (silo), 56 top; © Tom Bol, Chugiak, Ark.: 88 top; © C. Boylan/Unicorn Stock Photos, Kansas City, Mo.: 121 top; © Sonja Bullaty, New York: 88 bottom, 90, 97, 99 bottom, 100, 101 top, 101 bottom, 105 bottom, 109, 116, 117 top, 117 bottom; © Jane Burton/Bruce Coleman, U.K.: 3 (top silo), 12, 21 top, 21 bottom, 24 bottom, 39 top, 63 top, 69 (silo), 73, 79 top, 79 bottom, 119 (silo), 130, 134 bottom, 135 bottom; © Paul Butler, Los Angeles: 58 bottom, 64, 122, 123, 128 bottom; © Diane Calkins/Click the Photo Connection, Encinitas, Calif.: 3 (bottom silo), 50, 87 (silo), 91, 114, 131 (silo), 142; © Dick Canby/Positive Images, Andover, Mass.: 83 bottom; © Ron Charles/Uniphoto, Washington, D.C.: 120; © Jack Clark/Comstock, Inc., New York: 77 top; © Stuart Cohen/Comstock, Inc., New York: 52; © Patrick Cone, Oakley, Utah: 27, 65, 128 top; © Kathi Corder/Unicorn Stock Photos, Kansas City, Mo.: 74–75; © Wendy Cortesi, Washington, D.C.: 111; © Joel Dexter/Unicorn Stock Photos, Kansas City, Mo.: 28 top; © Towny

Dickinson/Comstock, Inc., New York: 23, 24 top, 37, 56 bottom, 78, 80 bottom, 85; © Tommy Dodson/Unicorn Stock Photos, Kansas City, Mo.: 77 bottom; © R. Edgar/Megapress, Montreal: 104; © Patricia Fabricant, New York: 115; © Laura Foggini, Boston, Mass.: 136; © C. P. George/H. Armstrong Roberts, Inc.: 42; © Alfred Gescheidt/Fifi Oscard Agency, New York: 13 (silo), 15 bottom; © Art Gingert/Comstock, Inc., New York: 44 top, 46, 48; © Grenet & Soumillard/Megapress, Montreal: 93, 118; © Julie Habel/H. Armstrong Roberts, Inc.: 28 bottom, 49 bottom; © Galyn C. Hammond, Monterey, Calif.: 92 bottom; © Ed Harp/Unicorn Stock Photos, Kansas City, Mo.: 58 top; © Dane Hockenbrock/Joe McDonald Photography, McClure, Pa.: 33 left; © Thomas Hovland/Grant Heilman Photography, Inc., Lititz, Pa.: 80 top; © Geoffrey Hutchinson/Tom Keller & Associates, New York: 81; © Mark Ippolito/Comstock, Inc., New York: 39 bottom; © Russ Kinne/Comstock, Inc., New York: 30, 31 bottom, 72 bottom; © Kent Knudson/Uniphoto, Washington, D.C.: 127; © Kotoh/Zefa/H. Armstrong Roberts, Inc.: 92 top; © J. M. Labat/Megapress, Montreal: 93; © Werner Layer/Bruce Coleman, U.K.: 51; © Larry Lefever/Grant Heilman Photography, Inc., Lititz, Pa.: 121 bottom, 133, 138 top; © Angelo Lomeo, New York: 2, 94 top, 102 top, 103, 108, 113 top, 126 top; © Bruce McClellan, West Simsbury, Conn.: 70–71, 84,

126 bottom; © Joe McDonald Photography, McClure, Pa.: 1 (silo), 16; © Jim Olive/Uniphoto, Washington, D.C.: 72 top; © Rich Pomerantz, Washington Depot, Conn.: 18, 49 top, 54, 55 (both); © Andy Price/Bruce Coleman, U.K.: 44 bottom; © Karen Ramsey, Vallejo, Calif.: 66; © F. Reginier-Barral, Paris: 47 bottom, 76; © Hans Reinhard/Bruce Coleman, U.K.: 7 (silo), 15 top, 17, 22, 25 bottom, 36, 29, 31 top, 57, 142 top, 143; © H. Armstrong Roberts, Inc.: 20, 141; © Cheyenne Rouse, Cardiff, Calif.: 60; © Joan Sage, King Ferry, N.Y.: 38; © Mae Scanlan, Washington, D.C.: back cover, 45; © Rosemary Shelton/Click the Photo Connection, Encinitas, Calif.: 139; © Frank Siteman/Uniphoto, Washington, D.C.: 36 top left; © Roger Smith/Vision Impact Photography, Youngstown, Fla.: 32, 33 right, 34, 35, 36 bottom, 47 top, 61, 62, 63 bottom, 67, 68, 125 top, 140; © Carlos Spaventa, New York: 89, 94 bottom, 86, 98, 99 top, 110, 112, 113 bottom, 124, 125 bottom, 135 top; © Irvin Taputuarai/Invincible Productions, San Francisco: 129; © Michael Thompson/Comstock, Inc., New York: 36 top right, 41; © Uniphoto, Washington, D.C.: 4, 6, 14, 137; © Les Van/Unicorn Stock Photos, Kansas City, Mo.: 138 bottom; © Doug Wilson/H. Armstrong Roberts, Inc.: 86; ©Steve Wylymz/Comstock, Inc., New York: 82; © D. Young/Unicorn Stock Photos, Kansas City, Mo.: 95.

Editor: Jeffrey Golick
Designer: Jordana Abrams
Picture Editor: Scott Hall
Production Manager: Vicki Russell

First edition
2 4 6 8 10 9 7 5 3

The Library of Congress has cataloged the Abbeville edition as follows:
Croke, Vicki.
Cats up close / by Vicki Croke. — 1st ed.
p.   cm.
Includes biographical references (p.   ).
ISBN 0-7892-0198-4 (Tiny Folio)
1. Cats. I. Title.
SR445.5.C74 1997
636.8—dc21   97-23691

Artabras ISBN 0-89660-092-0